Massachusetts
TROUBLEMAKERS
Rebels, Reformers, and Radicals from the Bay State

PAUL DELLA VALLE

Guilford, Connecticut

Text design by Libby Kingsbury
Photos by Paul Della Valle where not otherwise credited

Library of Congress Cataloging-in-Publication Data
Della Valle, Paul.
Massachusetts troublemakers : rebels, reformers, and radicals from the Bay State / Paul Della Valle.
p. cm.
ISBN 978-0-7627-4850-1
1. Massachusetts—Biography. 2. Revolutionaries—Massachusetts—Biography. 3. Social reformers—Massachusetts—Biography. 4. Radicals—Massachusetts—Biography. 5. Massachusetts—History—Anecdotes. I. Title.
CT240.D45 2009
920.0744—dc22
2008036952

Printed in the United States of America
10 9 8 7 6 5 4 3 2 1

To my loving parents,
Valo Della Valle and Peggy Dalton Della Valle

Augustus Saint-Gaudens statue of Robert Gould Shaw on Boston Common

Contents

Contents

Introduction

The genesis of this book occurred when I was a *Worcester Telegram & Gazette* reporter in Leominster, Massachusetts, in the 1980s and I'd buy my supper some evenings at a fast food joint on Route 13. Evergreen Cemetery is across the road, and if you look over the stone wall there you can see a 6-foot-high obelisk with Joe Palmer's face and the inscription "Persecuted for Wearing the Beard" carved into it. Intrigued, I read stories about Palmer that portrayed him as a nineteenth-century eccentric and left it at that.

Ten years later, in the late 1990s, I owned a small newspaper in a neighboring town and decided to write a feature on area oddities. I did some research on Palmer and found not just an eccentric, but a courageous contrarian. In the Bay State we call someone like Joe Palmer a real character—actually in the parlance of modern-day Massachusetts we'd say, "a wicked cahrectah."

And that got me to thinking about other "wicked cahrectahs" I had read about or heard about and realized there has never been a shortage of them in the Bay State. The thing is, history is written by the winners and the first winners in the Commonwealth were the Puritans and Pilgrims—self-righteous English colonists who killed the natives by spreading disease, who hanged witches, and who were the lingering reason we couldn't buy beer on Sundays until a few years ago. Thus, Miles Standish got a lot of ink but no one would ever describe him as a "cahrectah."

Still, Massachusetts has had plenty. We talk funny and don't always see things like the rest of the country. Bay Staters are the ones who fired the first shots in the Revolution, the ones who led the fight for the abolition of slavery and women's suffrage, and the only ones who voted as a state for George McGovern instead of Richard Nixon in 1972—and we all know how that turned out.

Like so many of the people of my generation in eastern Massachusetts, I grew up in a "mezzo e mezzo"—or "Garlic & Gaelic"—household, half Italian and half Irish. I remember my Irish maternal grandmother rhapsodizing about Boston's James Michael Curley because "The Mayor of the Poor" had given her retarded brother a pillow at the Fernald School in Waltham. "The man was a saint," my Nana would say, and it was only as an adult that I found out Curley was also something of a crook, and one of the great "cahrectahs" in Bay State history.

The more I researched, the more I admired these troublemakers—the wit of Thomas Morton, the patriotism of Sam Adams and Deborah Samson, the courage of David Walker and Robert Gould Shaw, the integrity of Henry David Thoreau and Major Taylor. I fell in love with Margaret Fuller, who reminded me of my wife, Karen, who, like Fuller, thinks she is· "wicked smaaaht." (I do too, honey.) Everything about idealistic Lucy Stone—whose dying words were "Make the world better"—makes me think of my daughter Jewel. As someone whose family has been impacted by depression and bipolar disorder, I send kisses across the universe to Dorothea Dix, who worked tirelessly on the mentally ill's behalf.

I remain amazed and touched by the heartbreaking tragedies these people suffered. Morton and Taylor—the first and last chapter subjects—both died broke. And anyone who thinks they might have preferred living back in the 1700s or

1800s has only to count the children and spouses so many of these people lost to tuberculosis and other diseases. Even in the early part of the twentieth century, seven of Curley's nine children died before him, including a daughter and son who suffered cerebral hemorrhages hours apart while talking on the same telephone.

The one thing all these "troublemakers" had in common—besides their connection to the Commonwealth and a birth date before 1900—was some kind of backbone. Even William Miller, the zealot who caused the Great Disappointment in 1844, died convinced he was right and that the end of the world was at hand.

I need to thank a few people: the folks at Globe Pequot who decided this was a book they wanted to publish; Gillian Belnap, who originally championed this project; my editors Allen Jones and Jess Haberman, who guided this book home; copy editor Joshua Rosenberg; Worcester County historian Al Southwick, who pointed me in the right direction for research; my late father-in-law, Phil Callahan, a great storyteller who loved to talk about history; and especially my wife, my kids and step-kids (Rocky and his wife, Michele, Jewel, Lisa, Rory, and Devin), and my golfing buddies who patiently listened every time I burst out with a newly discovered tidbit prefaced by "Did you know . . . ?"

Most of all I want to thank my twenty troublemakers, whose rare courage to go against the grain made getting to know each of them one of the great pleasures of my life.

1

The Lord of Misrule

Thomas Morton fell in love with Massachusetts the second he spied her unspoiled shores from the deck of the *Unity* in 1624.

The cavalier English adventurer and poet also loved putting self-righteous Puritan and Pilgrim noses "out of joynt," however, and, just like the class clown who can't help himself, his antics—not to mention his beer bashes—kept getting him into trouble.

In 1643, Morton was expelled from Massachusetts for the third time for calling Miles Standish, the Pilgrims' vertically challenged military hero, "Captain Shrimp," and for his efforts in trying to get the Puritans' Massachusetts Bay Colony charter revoked.

Of course, there had been previous exiles for "frisking togither" with Indian "lasses in beaver coats" fifteen years earlier, and for the parties around the Maypole that went on for days. But Morton so loved Massachusetts—and the good times he had here—that he kept coming back. In his writing, he called Massachusetts "Nature's Masterpiece," because when he first arrived onboard the *Unity* he thought he was in heaven.

"I do not thinke that in all the knowne world it could be parallel'd," he later wrote. "So many goodly groves of trees,

Nineteenth-century rendering of the Maypole at Ma-re Mount

dainty fine round rising hillucks . . . sweet crystal fountains, and cleare running streams . . . in fine meanders through the meads . . . Fowles in abundance, Fishes in multitudes . . . Millions of Turtle doves . . . pecking at the full ripe pleasant grapes."

He also found the Algonquin-speaking people who lived near the coast—including the few members of the Massachusetts tribe who had survived a 1616–1618 plague brought here by early European traders—among the most admirable people he had ever met, easygoing, generous to all, kind to one another, and especially good to the elderly.

By some accounts, Thomas Morton was a New Age sort of guy, ahead of his time by almost four hundred years. By other accounts, he was a criminal libertine.

One thing is certain. For more than twenty years in the first half of the seventeenth century, Morton was a man detested by many in colonial Massachusetts, a freedom-loving cavalier living between the austere Puritans and their equally dour allies, the Pilgrims.

The Pilgrims in Plymouth and the Puritans in the Massachusetts Bay Colony all subscribed to the Protestant reforms of the sixteenth century and both groups were committed to "Puritanism." They were all for freedom of religion—as long as it was their religion. They hated Catholics and Quakers and pagans and the French, and they were superstitious. The self-righteous Puritans and Pilgrims thought they were superior to the Native Americans in every way and that they had a God-given right to displace them.

The biggest difference between the two groups was that the Pilgrims were "Separatists" who wanted to break away from the Church of England. They were also mostly working-class people. The Puritans were more often from the upper class and better educated. They saw even less separation between church and state than the Pilgrims. The size of the colonies was also strikingly different. When the *Mayflower* arrived at Plymouth in December 1620, it carried 102 passengers, half of whom died in the first terrible winter. In 1640, the population of Plymouth Colony was still just 2,500, while that of Boston-based Massachusetts Bay had risen to 20,000.

Still, the Puritans and Pilgrims had more in common than they had differences. And one thing they had in common was their hatred of Thomas Morton.

By 1628, Morton had angered the Pilgrims in Plymouth and Weymouth and the Puritans in Naumkeag (Salem) by freeing his indentured servants, by partying for days on end with his followers and with Indian men and women around an eighty-foot Maypole, and by being far more successful in the fur trade than they were. He also called the Native Americans "more Christian" than the Pilgrims at Plymouth, which certainly ticked off the "Visible Saints," as they called themselves.

Since the Pilgrims and Puritans controlled Massachusetts from its beginning and thus shaped its personality for centuries to come—remember Boston's infamous blue laws that survived well into the twentieth century—most historians did not treat Morton kindly. They often painted him as a rebel, a lascivious rascal and—as the Pilgrim's governor William Bradford called him—a "thirstie murderer," a "traytor" who recklessly endangered the early colonists by selling guns to the Native Americans.

"The danger was indeed imminent," historian Charles Francis Adams wrote in *Three Episodes of Massachusetts History* in 1893. "It mattered little whether Morton realized what he was doing. . . . The infant settlements had quite as much to dread from the gathering scum of civilization [that would be Morton and his followers] as they ever had to dread from anything except sickness, fire and famine. . . . Those composing these settlements had come to New England to stay. They had bought with them their wives and children and were living at best in feeble communities on the verge of an unknown wilderness far removed from human protection."

Jack Dempsey, a Morton biographer and editor of a 1999 annotated version of Morton's book, *New English Canaan*, argues that the historians who bought the Puritan party line were unfair. Dempsey said Morton was actually much more in step with the prevailing liberal English values of his day than were his pious New World antagonists. Morton's skills in "cooperating" with the land and Native Americans, Dempsey wrote, led to a prosperous multicultural plantation that threatened the Pilgrims and Puritans economically. In his biography of Morton, which accompanies his edited *New English Canaan*, Dempsey wrote that Morton was doing business with the Native Americans the same way European traders had been doing it for a century, and the same way the Native Americans had been doing it among themselves for a millennium.

"Cohabitation with Native American women, the trade of contraband items between the races and cultures, and 'revelry' . . . had been normal components of life in the America now being shared by such radically different peoples," Dempsey wrote. "In Native American societies, as Morton's men would soon find, intertribal socializing, marriage and kinship were already the indispensable contexts of trade and material exchange. Fishermen and fur-traders had followed suit for 100 years, 'complying with [these] humors' in Morton's phrase for the ways of the peoples who controlled the land."

It was Morton's misfortune that the way things had been done for a century was changing rapidly due to the Pilgrims' and Puritans' conservative influence in England and the New World.

"Morton was a 'rebel' in only one sense; that his old-English and Renaissance values were struggling to flower in American soil among the peoples who danced and traded round his Maypole," Dempsey said.

Even Adams, who clearly was not a fan of Morton's behavior, gave the Bay State's first party animal some of his due. He noted Morton was a deft humorist and that he absolutely loved Massachusetts.

"That his moral character was decidedly loose is apparent from his own statements, and such religious views as he had must have been mixed in character; yet, withal, he was a close observer, and his strange incoherent rambling book contains one of the best descriptions of Indian life, traits and habits, and of the trees, products and animal life of New England, which has come down to us," Adams wrote. "The man had, in fact, an innate love of nature and, an Englishman's passion for field sports. What, except love of adventure, originally brought him to New England, is not likely to be known; but, when once he got there, he was never able to take himself off, nor could others drive him away."

Morton, a well-educated lawyer, first arrived in the New World in 1624, just four years after the Pilgrims, aka the Separatists, landed the *Mayflower* at Plymouth Rock. A partner in a trade expedition headed by a captain named Wollaston, Morton was immediately smitten. The adventurers settled in what is now part of the city of Quincy, just south of Boston and thirty miles north of Plymouth, and named it Mount Wollaston. After one winter, though, the captain had had enough of New England and left for Virginia. Morton took over and renamed the settlement Ma-re Mount [Merrymount], an intentional play on both the Latin word for sea and on the good times he and his freed indentured servants would soon be having there with their Native American pals. Both Wollaston and Merrymount survive as section names in Quincy today.

Morton's free spirit and partying really galled the Pilgrims, who spent much of their time in three-hour church services and other pious Calvinist pursuits. Governor Bradford included this account of Ma-re Mount in his *History of Plimoth Plantation:*

> *After this they fell to great licenciousnes, and led a dissolute life, powering out them selves into all profanenes. And Morton became lord of misrule, and maintained (as it were) a schoole of Athisme [Atheism]. And after they had gott some good into their hands, and gott much by trading with ye Indeans, they spent it as vainly, in quaffing & drinking both wine & strong waters in great exsess, and,*

as some reported, £10 worth in a morning. They allso set up a May-
pole, drinking and dancing aboute it many days togeather, inviting
the Indean women, for their consorts, dancing and frisking togither,
(like so many fairies, or furies rather).

The "frisking togither" wasn't the worst of it, though. By selling the Native Americans guns and making them trade partners, the self-dubbed "Hoste of Ma're Mount" had grabbed the lion's share of the New World's beaver pelt market. The final straw—or shall we say the first of several penultimate final straws—came in 1627 when Morton erected his Maypole with the inscription, "The first of May/At Ma-re Mount shall be kept holyday" attached to it. The party had begun.

"[We] therefore brewed a barrell of excellent beare and provided a case of bottles, to be spent, with other good cheare, for all commers of that day," Morton wrote in *New English Canaan*. He also included the lyrics to "the songe" they sang at the party: "Drinke and be merry, merry, merry boyes . . . Lasses in beaver coats come away, Yee shall be welcome to us night and day. To drinke and be merry."

That Morton's men would take up with native women should come as no surprise. No English women, except briefly for one poor soul Morton dubbed "the Barren Doe," lived in the Ma-re Mount settlement.

"Between work, drinking, and fighting, the trading post life along the New England coast from 1615 to 1640 offered little to attract wives or clergymen, but it appealed to men of courage in an age of adventure," according to Charles Knowles Bolton in his *The Real Founders of New England: Stories of Their Life along the Coast, 1602–1628*.

Ma-re Mount's multicultural good life was just too much for the Visible Saints in Plymouth to take. Just picture Bradford and the other Pilgrims lying awake night after night next to their righteous English wives fearing that someone somewhere was having a good time—with native women no less. In the summer of 1628, Bradford sent a squad of soldiers under

Captain Shrimp, who was as brutal as he was short, to arrest Morton. According to Standish's account, Morton and his pals were too drunk to put up a fight and Morton was captured. The charges included "abusing the Indian women most filthily, as it is notorious." Standish took Morton to the Isles of Shoals off the coast of New Hampshire and left him there, "without gunne, powder or shot, or dogge or so much as a knife," according to Morton. His Indian pals brought him food and provisions until he was shipped off to England a month later to face the charges. While he was gone, Puritan leader John Endicott marched down the coast from Salem and cut down the Maypole.

Nothing was done to Morton in England—he was friendly with poet Ben Jonson and other influential people— and soon he was back in Massachusetts. In 1630, John Winthrop, the governor of the rapidly growing Massachusetts Bay Colony—the great migration of English Puritans to Boston had begun—ordered Morton arrested again, sentenced him to the stocks, and had Ma-re Mount burned to the ground.

Morton was sent back to England—again. He was jailed without charges and then released without penalty—again. He stayed in England for a dozen years and wrote *New English Canaan*, published in 1637, extolling the beauty and bounty of Massachusetts and parodying the Puritans, Pilgrims, and Captain Shrimp with sharp satire and poetry.

While in England, Morton joined in an effort to get the Massachusetts Bay Colony charter revoked. The effort was successful in court but the result never enforced. His involvement cost him dearly, though, because Massachusetts still held Morton's heart. In 1643, at about seventy years old, Morton sailed once more across the Atlantic. He arrived to find most of his Native American friends dead, killed by colonists' guns or by disease. (Due mainly to smallpox and other deadly illnesses introduced by Europeans, the Native American population in southern New England dropped from between an estimated 80,000 to 140,000 people in 1615 to less than 20,000 in 1670.)

Although few of Morton's Native American friends were left when he returned, he did find one angry governor, thanks to his efforts to revoke the charter and to what he had written in *New English Canaan*. When Morton reappeared in Massachusetts, Winthrop noted in his journal that "our professed old adversary, who had set forth a book against us and had written reproachful and menacing letters to some of us" had arrived.

Winthrop ordered Morton thrown into jail, where he remained for the entire winter. He was then fined one hundred pounds and ordered out of Boston. He left for the wilds of the Maine coast, which was then sparsely settled and outside of the jurisdiction of the Massachusetts colony. According to Winthrop, Morton was "old and crazy" by then and lived "poor and despised" until his death in 1647.

Two centuries after Morton died, Nathaniel Hawthorne immortalized the struggle between New England's early freedom lover and the Puritans in a short story, "The May-Pole of Merry Mount." Dempsey said scholars now agree that Morton was "a first rate observer, a versatile writer," who produced one of the first true accounts of seventeenth-century New England. Because of the focus on his Maypole partying and a lingering Puritan influence, however, Morton was seldom treated fairly by researchers until the twentieth century turned toward the twenty-first and early assessments of the "Hoste of Mare-Mount" were revisited.

"He goes down as one of history's losers," wrote Massachusetts historian and author Albert B. Southwick in 2006. "But we, 360 years later, can cherish the memory of one of our land's first notable contrarians, a man who refused to be mentally confined by the harsh Calvinism of the time, a man who thought that life should be joyful as well as useful, and a man who loved New England with all his heart, mind and soul."

2

Anne Hutchinson, 1591–1643
America's First Feminist

The apple—or in this case the antinomian—didn't fall far from the family tree for Anne Hutchinson.

Born Anne Marbury in 1591 in Alford, England, she saw her father, the Reverend Francis Marbury, a deacon at Christ Church Cambridge, imprisoned for a year for his outspoken criticism of Church of England ministers.

In 1643, after being exiled from Massachusetts for the same offense against Puritan ministers five years earlier, Hutchinson was killed along with five of her children in an Indian massacre near Long Island Sound.

By then, she was the most notorious woman in the colonies, loved by some and loathed by others. Hutchinson is often called America's first feminist and it would be hard to argue against that suggestion. Just listen to the language of the Massachusetts Bay Colony's first governor, John Winthrop, in describing her: "If she had attended her household affairs, and such things as belong to women, and had not gone out of her way and calling to meddle in such things as are proper for men, whose minds are stronger, etc., she had kept her wits and might have improved them usefully and honorably in the place God had set her."

Or this description by another of her antagonists, the Reverend Thomas Weld: "Of a haughty and fierce carriage, of a nimble wit and an active spirit, and a very voluble tongue, more bold than a man."

More than just bold, Hutchinson was courageous. Despite threats of exile and excommunication, she would not back down from her critique of early Boston's religious leaders or her claim of divine revelations. She was brilliant and well spoken, and even Winthrop's biographer said she got the best of the governor and her other male accusers during her trial.

Another thing that can't be argued is her progeny's role in American politics from colonial times to today. Anne Hutchinson's great-great-grandson Thomas Hutchinson was the last royal governor of Massachusetts. President George W. Bush is a direct descendant of Hutchinson, according to Hutchinson biographer Eve LaPlante (*American Jezebel*), who is also a direct descendant of Hutchinson. So is former Massachusetts governor Mitt Romney. Massachusetts senator John F. Kerry, Bush's opponent in the 2004 presidential election, is a descendant of Winthrop.

Today, a bronze statue of Hutchinson and her daughter Susannah stands outside the Massachusetts Statehouse in Boston. The inscription says, "In Memory of Anne Marbury Hutchinson, Courageous Exponent of Civil Liberty and Religious Toleration." The placement of the statue is ironic, because she was so reviled by the powerful men in seventeenth-century Boston that when Indians killed her and her children, many considered it God's judgment.

"A most heavy stroak upon herself and hers," Weld wrote. "Some write that the Indians did burn her to death with fire, her house and the rest named that belonged to her; but I am not able to affirm what kind of death slew her, but slain it seems she is according to all reports. I never heard that the Indians in those parts did ever before commit the like outrage upon any one family or families; and therefore God's hand is the more apparently seen herein, to pick this woful woman, to make her and those belonging to her an unheard of heavy example of their cruelty above others."

Susannah was the only one of the sixteen people in the house not killed that day. The attacking Mohegans spared the ten-year-old girl from their blades because she had red hair. They raised her for a time before returning her to the colonists.

Anne Hutchinson was so reviled by Winthrop and the other Puritan preachers that she was initially forced to stand at her trial in 1637, even though she was pregnant for the sixteenth time. Winthrop, a compulsive diarist, called her an "ally of Satan" and "an American Jezebel." Following her conviction, she was held for months in house arrest until her excommunication hearing, pretty much a foregone conclusion after the guilty verdict at the civil trial. The colony's preachers took turns attacking her during the excommunication hearing. The minister of Salem shouted at her, "You have stepped out of your place. You have rather been a husband than a wife, and a preacher than a hearer."

Finally, another Boston Puritan preacher, John Wilson, who Hutchinson had often crossed, excommunicated her with these words.

"I doe cast you out and in the name of Christ. I doe deliver you up to Satan, that you may learne no more to blaspheme, to seduce, and to lye. . . . I command you in the name of Jesus Christ and of this church, as a leper to withdraw yourself out of the congregation."

"The Lord judgeth not as man judgeth," Hutchinson responded. "Better to be cast out of the church than to deny Christ."

As Hutchinson left the church, only her friend Mary Dyer, who like Hutchinson had once given birth to a stillborn, deformed baby, walked with her. One onlooker pointed to Dyer and called out, "It is the woman which had the monster." Dyer, who was also banished for supporting her friend, later returned to Massachusetts and was hanged on Boston Common in 1660 for espousing Quakerism.

What could Hutchinson, a perennially pregnant midwife, have done to deserve such wrath?

Basically she could think, she had opinions and she could speak well, and worst of all, she had become immensely popular—with many men as well as women—in Boston. She had disagreed with the preachers on a central point of Puritan doctrine. She argued that men and women could be saved by a covenant of grace (predestination for heaven) alone. She said the Holy Spirit had touched her and she claimed Wilson and other Puritan preachers practiced a covenant of works (meaning good deeds and adherence to rigid religious laws were required for salvation).

It is important to remember here that the Puritans in the Massachusetts Bay Colony effectively believed in little separation of church and state—the Bible was the source for all law—and they also believed in a powerful and vengeful God. They lived a dire existence, believing every wrong thing they did, even offenses of little consequence, directly caused more bad things, such as the bloody Pequot War of 1637, to happen here on Earth.

"A father, industrious or interested in his task, works one hour after Saturdays sunset, and the next day his little child of five years is drowned, and he sees in his misfortune only the 'the righteous hand of God, for profaning His holy day against the checks of his own conscience,'" historian Charles Francis Adams wrote in 1893 about the seventeenth-century Boston Puritans. "And when the most terrible misfortune incident to maternity befell Anne Hutchinson and her friend, the no less unhappy Mary Dyer, the grave magistrates and clergy, gloating in blasphemous words over each lying detail of the monstrous fruit of their wombs, saw therein, 'God Himself bring in his own vote and suffrage from heaven.'"

The Puritans also believed in witches, as witnessed by the 1692 trials in Salem, and they were, much like their God, brutal and vengeful. Even their Mohegan and Narragansett allies were aghast when Puritan military leaders ordered a stockade containing five hundred to seven hundred Pequot men, women, and children set afire in Mystic, Connecticut, during the Pequot War. Puritan captain John Underhill, writing later, couldn't understand the criticism.

"It may be demanded, 'Why should you be so furious?'" he wrote. "'Should not Christians have more mercy and compassion?' Sometimes the Scripture declareth women and children must perish with their parents. Sometimes the case alters, but we will not dispute it now. We had sufficient light from the word of God for our proceedings."

The word of God indeed. The Puritans in Boston—in 1634 a community of two thousand people but exponentially growing—had no entertainment other than debating the minutiae of their religion. Freedom of religion, not the opportunity that would bring so many others to America in subsequent centuries, was the reason they had left the Old World for the new. But their version of freedom of religion was hardly what the framers of the Declaration of Independence had in mind a century and a half later. The Puritans in Salem and Boston and the Pilgrims (or Separatists as they were called in the seventeenth century) who landed forty miles to the south of Boston in Plymouth had no desire that others could worship as they wished. They only cared about the freedom of *their* religion, which, especially in the Puritans' case, governed all aspects of their society. Winthrop was not only the governor, he was also a preacher. And unlike the Pilgrims, who believed in somewhat greater separation of church and state, the Puritans believed that once elected, their leaders ruled with divine authority.

The verbiage expended in the covenant of grace versus covenant of works debate seems mind-boggling today, as it did even to Adams in the nineteenth century.

"The real difficulty lay in the fact that words and phrases to which they attached an all-important significance did not admit of definition and consequently were devoid of exact meaning," Adams wrote. "They were simply engaged in hot wrangling over the unknowable."

Hutchinson married her husband William in England in 1612 when she was twenty-one and immediately started having babies. In 1634, William and Anne and their children sailed to Boston on the *Griffin*, following Puritan minister John Cotton of Boston, England, to the "new Boston" in the Massachusetts Bay Colony. The *Griffin* also carried cattle requested by Massachusetts governor John Winthrop. During the two-month journey across the Atlantic, Anne told her fellow passengers she had had revelations. A preacher on board, Zachariah Symmes, heard her and when they landed warned church officials that she would be a problem. He was correct.

Soon after arriving, Hutchinson, then forty-three, began holding weekly meetings in her home to discuss church sermons. At first only women came to discuss the previous Sunday's sermons given by Cotton or Wilson, but before long Anne began adding in her own beliefs. Then men, including a young Henry Vane, began to go to Mistress Anne's meetings, which took on a new importance as they transformed into heated discussions. Soon Hutchinson claimed most of the ministers in Boston were practicing a covenant of works and that only two Boston ministers were "elect" or saved, John Cotton and her brother-in-law, John Wheelwright. By then Hutchinson had attracted a huge following, and she wielded considerable influence when Vane became governor in 1636.

When Hutchinson, with the aid of Vane and Cotton, tried to have her brother-in-law installed as the associate minister of the Boston church, most of the congregation supported her. But a schism soon developed, Vane lost his office to Winthrop and Winthrop became determined to silence Hutchinson. She was branded as a heretic and antinomian—one who believes Christians are not bound by moral law. That was not technically true, but the antinomian label stuck and for centuries Hutchinson's case has been called the Antinomian Controversy.

In November 1637, Winthrop filed charges against Hutchinson and Wheelwright. Wheelwright was tried first and banished. He ended up moving to what is now New Hampshire. Hutchinson was then tried in what is now Cambridge

Illustration from *Harper's Monthly,* 1901

for "traducing" (slandering) the ministers, disobeying the fifth commandment by disobeying the fathers of the colony, and for other behavior "not fitting for her sex."

The two-day trial went well for Hutchinson at first. Pregnant, standing, and without counsel, Hutchinson parried every question from her accusers and from the forty-three-man court which Winthrop, a trained lawyer, had appointed and presided over. Edmund S. Morgan, a biographer of Winthrop's, later wrote that Hutchinson was the governor's "intellectual superior in everything except political judgment; in everything except the sense of what was possible in this world."

But then, out of the blue and without prodding, Hutchinson told the court she had had revelations. Jesus Christ revealed himself to her, she said, "upon a Throne of Justice." She then added a threat, according to a transcript of the trial printed by her great-great-grandson, royal governor Thomas Hutchinson, in his *History of the Colony and Province of Massachusetts.*

Anne Hutchinson: *Ever since that time I have been confident of what he hath revealed unto me . . . Therefore I desire you to look to it, for you see this scripture fulfilled this day and therefore I desire you that as you tender the Lord and the church and commonwealth to consider and look what you do. You have power over my body but the Lord Jesus hath power over my body and soul, and assure yourselves thus much, you do as much as in you lies to put the Lord Jesus Christ from you, and if you go on in this course you begin you will bring a curse upon you and your posterity, and the mouth of the Lord hath spoken it. . . .*

Governor Winthrop: *The court hath already declared themselves satisfied concerning the things you hear, and concerning the troublesomeness of her spirit and the danger of her course amongst us, which is not to be suffered. Therefore if it be the mind of the court that Mrs. Hutchinson for these things that appear before us is unfit for our society, and if it be the mind of the court that she shall be banished out of our liberties and imprisoned till she be sent away,* *let them hold up their hands. [All but three of the forty-three men did.]*

Mrs. Hutchinson, the sentence of the court you hear is that you are banished from out of our jurisdiction as being a woman not fit for our society, and are to be imprisoned till the court shall send you away.

Anne Hutchinson: *I desire to know wherefore I am banished?*

Governor: *Say no more, the court knows wherefore and is satisfied.*

Hutchinson spent the winter in house arrest. On March 15, 1638, her excommunication trial started. By then, even Reverend Cotton had turned against her, calling her co-ed meetings a, "promiscuous and filthie coming together of men and women without Distinction of Relation of Marriage. . . . Your opinions frett like a Gangrene and spread like a Leprosie, and will eate out the very Bowells of Religion."

She was excommunicated and banished from Massachusetts.

"Proud Jezebel has at last been cast down," Winthrop wrote.

Hutchinson, along with her husband William, their children, Dyer, and about sixty other followers went south (following clergyman Roger Williams who had been banished earlier, mainly for denouncing the Puritans' union of church and state). The Hutchinsons purchased land from the Narragansetts, and Anne, along with William Coddington, established the community that today is Portsmouth, Rhode Island.

William Hutchinson died in 1642. Anne, upon hearing rumors that the Massachusetts Bay Colony would soon attempt to take control of Rhode Island, took her six youngest children to what is now Pelham Bay, a section of the Bronx in New York.

The Dutch in the nearby New Amsterdam settlement had been harassing area Native Americans for years, and finally the

Indians rose up in 1643 and attacked settlements beyond the walled protection of New Amsterdam. Anne's family's home was attacked by a band of Mohegans in August 1643 and she was slaughtered with fifteen other people in the house, including five of her children. Susannah was captured and raised for two years by the Native Americans.

"When another treaty of peace was finally concluded with the Indians in 1645, one of the articles insisted on was a solemn obligation to restore the daughter of Anne Hutchinson," Winnifred King-Rugg wrote in her 1930 book, *Unafraid: A Life of Anne Hutchinson*. "The Dutch guaranteed the ransom that had been offered by the New England friends of the little captive, and the obligation on both sides was fulfilled. Susan was restored to the Dutch—against her will, it is said, since she had learned to like her Indian captors—and she was eventually returned to Rhode Island."

In the 1971 biography, *Eleanor and Franklin*, Joseph P. Lash wrote that Eleanor Roosevelt began her list of America's greatest women with Anne Hutchinson.

3

---◆---

Metacom, aka King Philip,
1638–1676
The George Washington of Native Americans

K ing Philip's War, which raged for fifteen months in 1675
and 1676, was—proportional to population—the bloodiest
war in American history, and undoubtedly the most vicious.

Fueled by desperation and righteous resentment, a coali-
tion of Algonquin tribes led by Metacom, aka King Philip,
attacked nearly half of the English towns in New England.
Twenty-five towns, including thirteen in the Plymouth and
Massachusetts Bay colonies, were destroyed and abandoned.
More than six hundred colonists were killed during the war
and at least six thousand Indians, about one third of the native
population in southern New England, died or were sold into
slavery.

The eventual English victory ended organized Native
American resistance to the colonization of southern New England. Although Indians in Maine and New Hampshire continued fighting for more than a year after Metacom died, and
sporadic Indian attacks continued on frontier towns throughout all of New England for decades, the once robust Indian
presence in Massachusetts was obliterated. During the war,
Christian Indians and other noncombatant Native Americans
could be shot on sight if spotted outside of five "praying towns"

in eastern and central Massachusetts. After the war, thousands of Massachusetts natives were executed or sold into slavery in the West Indies, and colonists made many young Indian orphans slaves in their households.

Unspeakable cruelties on both sides marked the war. The Indians regularly scalped and cut up colonists they killed, and displayed their victims' body parts as trophies. They hacked off fingers to make necklaces and stripped skin from dead colonists for belts. When King Philip was killed by an Indian ally of the English—shot through the heart with a musket ball on August 12, 1676—the Puritans quartered him and cut his hands and head off. They sent his hands to Boston and carried his head into Plymouth colony on a pole, where it was displayed for more than twenty-five years.

How did Metacom go from being a celebrated son of Massasoit, the Pilgrims' savior, to the most vilified man in the colonies? And why, 150 years later, was he revisited as a George Washington–like figure in many circles? He even became the glorified subject of a controversial hit show performed by the leading actor of the mid-nineteenth century. Today, King Philip is memorialized in Massachusetts by a highway, a high school, and many enterprises that bear his name.

The answer to the first question lies in the fifty-five years after Massasoit, sachem of the Pocasset-Wampanoag, helped the Pilgrims through their first brutal winter upon their arrival in Plymouth. Massasoit is still often featured in children's plays about the first Thanksgiving that followed in 1621. The Pilgrims called Massasoit the "king" of the Indians and they called his two sons, whose Indian names were Wamsutta and Metacom, Alexander and Philip after the ancient Macedonian leaders.

"We have found the Indians very faithful in their covenant of peace with us, very loving, and ready to pleasure us," Pilgrim leader Edward Winslow wrote. "We often go to them, and they come to us . . . we, for our part, walk as peaceably and safely in the wood as in the highways in England."

PHILLIP alias METACOMET of Pokanoket.

Engraved from the original as Published by Church.

Print from an engraving by Paul Revere of Metacom

That changed, though, as the Pilgrims, and especially the Puritans who soon came in great numbers, began mistreating the natives based on an ideology of racial superiority. By the time he died in 1662, Massasoit's friendship with the English had become smoldering hostility. Massasoit had seen the English time and again swindle the Indians out of their land and he had witnessed many thousands of natives succumbing to smallpox and other diseases brought to the Massachusetts coast by the whites.

In fact, tens of thousands of Native Americans in southern New England had died in a 1616–1618 plague introduced by European traders even before the Pilgrims arrived. The Native American population in southern New England is thought to have been between 80,000 and 140,000 people prior to 1615, and by 1670 it had been reduced to less than 20,000. Winslow described seeing acres and acres of untended cornfields on the first Pilgrim expedition outside of Plymouth in the summer of 1621. Thousands of "sculs and bones were found in many places," he wrote, "lying still above the ground, where their houses and dwellings had been; a very sad spectackle to behold."

Because of steadily increasing English emigration to the New World and native decimation due to disease, the white population in New England is believed to have more than doubled the native population by 1670.

After Massasoit's death, relations between the colonists and Native Americans worsened. The Pequot of Connecticut had been almost wiped out during a war in 1637, and colonists in New England lived in great fear that the Wampanoag, the Narragansett, the Nipmuc, and other tribes would also rise up. Their fears were well founded as the Native Americans, especially the Wampanoag, were privately talking about war.

Before the year 1662 was out, Plymouth leaders summoned Alexander, who became sachem of the Wampanoag upon Massasoit's death, to explain the rumors of war. He refused to go to Plymouth and had to be forcibly escorted to the meeting. He mysteriously died as he returned home days later, probably, as Philip believed, because he had been poisoned.

Philip assumed leadership of the Wampanoag upon Alexander's death and the talk of war grew louder on both sides. It was essentially all about territory and racism. The Reverend Increase Mather at that time described King Philip as one of the "heathen people amongst whom we live, and whose Land the Lord God of our Fathers hath given to us for a rightful Possession."

Many years later, his son the Reverend Cotton Mather, slave owner and apologist for the Salem witch trials, would describe the illnesses that had decimated the New England tribes as blessings from God. "The woods were almost cleared of those pernicious creatures, to make room for a better growth," Cotton Mather wrote. Even a century later, the British in America were intent on using germ warfare against the native peoples. In 1763, Lord Jeffery Amherst, commanding general of the British forces during the French and Indian War, wrote that he favored a plan to provide smallpox-infected blankets to Native Americans and "to try Every other method that can serve to Extirpate this Execrable Race." (Ironically, the town of Amherst, which is named after the general, is a bastion of diversity and liberalism today and home to several institutions of higher learning, including the University of Massachusetts. At well-endowed Amherst College, the sports teams are inexplicably nicknamed "the Lord Jeffs.")

Tension between the growing white population and the dwindling Indian population remained high through the 1660s and into the 1670s. In January 1675, the body of a Christian Indian named Sassamon was found in a pond near Plymouth. Sassamon had fought on the English side in the Pequot War. He had failed in his attempt to convert Philip to Christianity and was, perhaps, murdered for telling the colonists of Philip's preparations for war. Three of Philip's Wampanoag friends were tried and convicted of the murder and hanged on June 8.

Relations between the English and the Algonquin peoples were a tinderbox and on June 24, 1675, just weeks after the hangings, the fuse was lit. Wampanoag warriors killed seven colonists in Swansea in retaliation for the killing of an Indian by an English farmer. The farmer had killed the Indian because the Wampanoag had slaughtered some English cattle and destroyed three farms after the cattle trampled their cornfields. The Swansea killings are most often considered the beginning of King Philip's War. The conflict would soon involve every New England colony and all of the Algonquin tribes.

"From the firing of the first shots, both sides pursued the war with viciousness, and almost without mercy," Jill Lepore wrote in her 1998 book, *The Name of War*.

Philip declared his intention to make a stand.

"I am determined not to live until I have no country," he warned the whites.

Within fourteen months, the Narragansett, Nipmuc, Pocomtuck, and Wampanoag had reduced thirteen towns in the Plymouth and Massachusetts Bay colonies to ashes. English militia, led by their Pequot and Mohegan allies, scoured the swamps and forests to search out and kill Philip's followers. Both sides regularly killed women and children, and torture and mutilation were the order of the day.

In July and August 1675, Philip's confederation laid waste to Middleborough, Mendon, Dartmouth, Plymouth, and Brookfield, all in eastern or central Massachusetts. In the fall, they attacked Deerfield, Springfield, Hatfield, and Northampton in the west. During the winter, the confederation attacked and burned Lancaster, Medfield, Groton, Longmeadow and Marlborough, as well as Providence and Pawtucket in Rhode Island, and Simsbury in Connecticut. In the spring, five hundred Nipmucs sacked Sudbury, just twenty miles from Boston.

Colonists were petrified. After each battle, the Native Americans would "co-hoop" the number of enemy dead, a loud, chilling spectacle designed to frighten the survivors. In a letter about the attack on Marlborough, colonist Richard Jacobs wrote the Indians "began to signifie to us how many were slaine. They Cohooped sevnty-four times, which we hoped was only to affright us."

After the attack on Medfield, in which thirty colonists were killed or taken captive and fifty houses destroyed, one of the Nipmuc warriors posted a note on a tree that warned, "we care not though we war with you this 21 years . . . we hauve nothing but our lives to loose but thou hast many faire houses cattell & much good things."

The Puritans were convinced the Indians were the manifestation of the devil and also that the war was caused by their own sins. (The Indians enjoyed mocking the Puritans' zealotry: During the attack on Sudbury, Nipmuc warriors chased an elderly unarmed man into a swamp and before killing him one shouted, "Come Lord Jesus, save this poor Englishman if thou canst, whom I am now about to kill.")

Driven by fear and by a belief in their racial and moral superiority, the colonists proved just as vicious. Indians not taking part in the war were promised safe haven and instead sold into slavery if they were young and fit, or executed if they were old and feeble. The Massachusetts Bay Council exiled two hundred of the peaceful Christian Indians of Natick to Deer Island in Boston Harbor in the winter of 1675–1676 where they were ordered not to cut any wood or harm the sheep there. Many died of starvation, exposure, and disease. The colonial fighting men regularly disobeyed stated policy by destroying the Christian Indians' corn and other food supplies.

Some Puritans, but not many, were horrified by how vicious they themselves had become. The Reverend John Eliot, who had spent many years converting Indians to Christianity, decried the selling of native men, women, and children into slavery.

"This usage of them is worse than death," Eliot wrote to the Massachusetts Bay governor and council. "The design of

Christ in these last dayes is not to extirpate nations but to gospelize them."

The most vicious decision by the colonists was also a strategically poor one. In December 1675, they staged a preemptive attack on the Narragansett tribe, which had signed a peace treaty. The massacre in the Great Swamp of Rhode Island, where hundreds of Indian men, women, and children were killed—many burned alive inside their wigwams or bludgeoned as they fled from the wooden fort the colonists had set on fire—brought the Narragansett full force into the war on Philip's side.

The Agawam tribe in Western Massachusetts had also been living in peace with the colonists but joined Philip after settlers took some of their children as hostages as a precautionary move against an attack. The enraged Agawams burned 30 homes to the ground in an attack on Springfield. Mary Rowlandson, the wife of the minister of Lancaster, was taken captive with her six-year-old daughter when their garrison was attacked in February 1676. Her account, *The Sovereignty and Goodness of God*, which includes several meetings with Philip himself, became the first bestseller written in America and helped set an image of Native Americans that the English, and even Hollywood moviemakers, would ascribe to for centuries. Rowlandson, whose baby died in her arms during the attack and who saw many of her relatives crawling in pools of their own blood outside the burning garrison, described the Nipmuc warriors as "hellhounds" and "heathens." Her daughter succumbed to her wounds during the first month of captivity. Rowlandson became the property of King Philip's sister and brother-in-law and spent three months with her captors as they roamed through central and western Massachusetts and southern Vermont. Constant movement allowed the Indians to avoid the English militias throughout the war, but it also led to their downfall as they could not plant, tend, or harvest corn and other crops and they soon ran out of food.

During her captivity, Rowlandson witnessed many instances of cruelty but also many acts of kindness from her captors. Several times, Rowlandson met Metacom, whom she described as "a crafty fox."

"Then I went to see King Philip," she wrote. "He bade me come in and sit down, and asked me whether I would smoke. . . . During my abode in this place, Philip spake to me to make a shirt for his boy, which I did, for which he gave me a shilling. I offered the money to my master, but he bade me keep it; and with it I bought a piece of horseflesh. Afterwards he asked me to make a cap for his boy, for which he invited me to dinner. I went, and he gave me a pancake, about as big as two fingers. It was made of parched wheat, beaten, and fried in bear's grease, but I thought I never tasted pleasanter meat in my life."

By the spring of 1676, King Philip's alliance began to fall apart. The Narragansetts were decimated in one battle, the Nipmucs in another. In January, Philip had traveled to Mohawk territory in what is now upstate New York, unsuccessfully seeking to enlist their aid. The Mohawks, traditional enemies of many of the tribes involved in the conflict, instead began attacking the Indians allied with Philip. Many of the Indians who had joined Philip drifted into New Hampshire, Vermont, and Canada. Some joined the Abenaki in Maine, who were also fighting colonists there.

In July 1676, Philip retreated to Mount Hope, Rhode Island. On August 1, his wife and nine-year-old son were captured, much to the delight of the Reverend Increase Mather:

"His Squaw and his Son were taken Captives and are now Prisoners in Plimouth," wrote Mather in his *An History of the Warr with Indians in New England* published that same year. "Thus has God brought that grand Enemy into great misery before he quite destroy him. It must needs to be bitter as death to him, to loose his Wife and only Son (for the Indians are marvellous fond and affectionate toward their Children)." Most historians believe Philip's wife and son were later sold into slavery in the Caribbean.

In early August, Philip's sister-in-law Weetamoo, who had been married to Wamsutta and who had herself become a leader in the war, drowned in the Taunton River while fleeing militia. Her body was dismembered and her head put on display.

"When it was set upon a pole in Taunton, the Indians who were prisoners there knew it presently and made a most horrid and diabolical Lamentation, crying out it was their Queen's head," Increase Mather wrote. "Now here it is to be observed, that God Himself by his own hand, brought this enemy to destruction. For in that place, where the last year, she furnished Philip with Canooes for his men, she her self could not meet with a Canoo, but venturing over the River upon a Raft, that brake under her, so that she was drowned, just before the English found her. Surely Philip's turn will be next."

It was. On August 12, John Alderman, an Indian serving with Colonial leader Captain Benjamin Church, shot and killed Philip. The war in southern New England—and the Native Americans' way of life there—was over. Many Indians in Massachusetts were promised amnesty and then executed or sold into slavery. In July 1677, the wives of Marblehead fishermen used sticks and stones to beat to death Abenaki prisoners who had been captured in the continued fighting along the Maine coast. By 1812, in a letter to Thomas Jefferson, John Adams wrote of Massachusetts, "We scarcely see an Indian in a year." Most of the remaining four hundred Wampanoags settled in Mashpee on Cape Cod.

In the early nineteenth century, the anti-Indian sentiment began to change as Easterners, free from concern about attacks, began reassessing Metacom and King Philip's War. Guilt came into play.

Washington Irving in 1814 wrote "Philip of Pokanoket," which lauded Metacom as America's first patriot.

"Philip, in Irving's estimation, was a courageous leader struggling to free his people from the foreign tyranny embodied by colonial authorities," Lepore wrote.

In 1829, America's greatest actor, Edwin Forrest, began starring in a smash hit play called *Metamora* that ended with the line "My curses upon you, white men." Forrest played Metamora in American cities for more than two decades, with most white audiences in the East eating it up. The play nearly caused riots, however, in Georgia, where Cherokee removal was an ongoing controversy.

In perhaps the greatest stroke of irony, in February 2007, the federal government recognized the Mashpee Wampanoags as a tribe and nine months later a town meeting in Middleborough, one of the first towns that King Philip's warriors attacked and destroyed, voted to allow the Wampanoag to build a casino there.

4

───────◆◆◆───────

Samuel Adams, 1722–1803
The MVP (Most Valuable Propagandist)
of the New England Patriots

S am Adams failed as a businessman, brewer, and bread-
winner. Tragedy marked his family life—four of his five
children and his first wife died before him. But it is he—not
George Washington, Thomas Jefferson, nor his cousin John
Adams—who some consider to be the greatest hero of the
American Revolution.

Jefferson called Sam Adams "truly the man of the Revolution." John Adams, our second president, also gave his cousin
the credit. "Without [Sam Adams] in my opinion, American
independence could not have been declared in 1776," he wrote.

Through the years, many historians have agreed.

"Among those who signed the Declaration of Independence, and were conspicuous in the revolution, there existed, of
course, a great diversity of intellectual endowments," wrote the
Reverend Charles A. Goodrich in his book *Lives of the Signers
to the Declaration of Independence,* published in 1829. "Like the
luminaries of heavens each contributed his portion of influence; but, like them, they differed, as star differeth from star
in glory. But in the constellation of great men, which adorned
that era, few shone with more brilliancy, or exercised a more
powerful influence, than Samuel Adams."

PAINTED BY COPLEY.   ENGRAVED BY C. GOODMAN & R. PIGGOT.

SAMUEL ADAMS.

Samuel Adams

Gary Scott Smith, author of *Faith and the Presidency: From George Washington to George W. Bush,* wrote in a 2007 essay, "The Indispensable Man" that although Adams had achieved little in his first forty-two years of life, few ever gave so much for a cause and few cared so little about personal recognition or gain.

"More than any other American, Adams made the Revolution happen," Smith wrote. "'Would you believe,' a British officer wrote in 1775, 'that this immense continent, from New England to Georgia, is moved and directed by one man!—a man of ordinary birth and desperate fortune?' Adams, the officer complained, had used his 'talent for factious intrigue;' to foment revolution. . . . Some New England Tories denounced Adams as the 'grand Incendiary' who ignited the colonial conflagration, and labeled Boston's resistance the 'Adams conspiracy.'"

Washington, Jefferson, John Adams—even Patrick Henry and Lafayette—are probably more connected today to the founding of the nation in the American psyche than Samuel Adams. His name and image today are most associated with the popular beers and ales named after him. The truth is that Sam Adams' neglect helped make a mess of the family brewing business well before the Revolution, and—in maybe the greatest slight of all—the stein-holding patriot pictured on the Samuel Adams beer bottles' labels is actually based on a John Singleton Copley portrait of Paul Revere.

Writing and politics, not business affairs or accumulating family wealth, were Sam Adams's passions. Described by his cousin as "a plain, simple, decent citizen, of middling stature, dress and manners," Sam Adams was equally at home in a church or saloon. He made Boston's Green Dragon Tavern his headquarters before the Revolution and conversed as easily with shipyard workers and mechanics as he did with merchants and deacons.

And always he wrote.

"Every dip of his pen," royal governor Francis Bernard later recalled, "stung like a horned snake."

Through his prolific writings, speeches, and political activity—he was elected a member of the colony's legislature in 1765—Adams whipped Massachusetts and eventually the other colonies into a frenzy over British attempts to tax American trade through a series of economic bills, including the Sugar Act, Stamp Act, Townshend Acts, and Tea Act.

"If our trade may be taxed, why not our lands?" Adams wrote. "Why not the produce of our lands, and every thing we possess, or use? This we conceive annihilates our charter rights to govern and tax ourselves. It strikes at our British privileges, which, as we have never forfeited, we hold in common with our fellow subjects, who are natives of Britain. If taxes are laid upon us in any shape, without our having a legal representation, where they are laid, we are reduced from the character of free subjects to the state of tributary slaves."

In 1768, when British troops occupied Boston in reaction to the city's insolence—including the ransacking of royal governor Thomas Hutchinson's home by a drunken mob—Adams became the first colonial leader to talk openly about independence as the solution. Adams organized the Committee of Correspondence, which became a template for patriots in other colonies. His widely read published missives about British soldiers not respecting the Sabbath, beating young boys, and raping Boston women contributed to the hatred of British troops that led to the Boston Massacre of 1770, when British soldiers opened fire on colonists who were throwing snowballs and taunting them. Five colonists were killed. An outraged Sam Adams stepped up his call for Britain to pull all of its troops out of Boston. Ironically, cousin John Adams was the lawyer appointed for the accused soldiers and won an acquittal for the commander who ordered them to fire.

The British, knowing that Sam Adams had failed as a brewer and was somewhat destitute—the Tories derisively called him "Sam The Malster"—even tried to bribe him in 1773 to stop his political activities. According to Goodrich, Adams responded: "Go tell Governor Gage, that my peace has long since been made with the King of kings, and that it is the advice of Samuel Adams to him, no longer to insult the feelings of an already exasperated people." Everything about Sam Adams screamed love of country. Even his dog, a big Newfoundland named Queue, according to Adams' biographer James K. Hosmer, "appreciated perfectly what was expected of him as the dog of Sam Adams."

"[Queue] had a vast antipathy to the British uniform," Hosmer wrote. "He was cut and shot in several places by soldiers, in retaliation for his own sharp attacks, for the patriotic Queue anticipated the 'embattled farmers' of Concord Bridge in inaugurating hostilities, and bore to his grave honourable scars from his fierce encounters."

Adams's first wife Elizabeth died after eight years of marriage. Only two of their five children lived to become adults. Still Adams pressed on. He lost the family business and became a tax collector, mismanaging his accounts because he was a soft touch for a hard-luck story and he had to pay back eight thousand pounds. Still he pressed on. He founded a magazine that collapsed after one year. He wrote hundreds of letters calling for justice under British law (and eventually for freedom) to the *Boston Gazette* and other periodicals under at least twenty-five pen names. He was always broke. He continued to press on.

"Without the character of Samuel Adams, the true history of the American Revolution can never be written," John Adams wrote in 1817. "For 50 years, his pen, his tongue, his activity, were constantly exerted for his country without fee or reward."

After his election to the House of Representatives in 1765, Sam Adams became the leader of the radical party that soon controlled the Massachusetts Legislature. But nothing in his writings from the next three years argued for independence. In a letter he drafted for the Massachusetts Assembly in early 1768, he wrote that the people of Massachusetts were "so sensible . . . of this happiness and safety, in their union with, and dependence upon, the mother country, that they would by no means be inclined to accept of an independency, if offered to them."

That was before the British troops occupied Boston. The following year, in an article signed "Alfred" in the *Boston Gazette*, he wrote that the jealousy between the mother country and the colonies might collapse "the most glorious Empire the sun ever shone upon" and continued to rail at Britain's heavy-handed treatment of the colonies even after the Stamp Act was repealed.

"The Stamp Act was like a sword that Nero wished for, to have decollated the Roman People at a stroke, or like Job's Sea monster," he wrote to a friend in South Carolina. "The Sight of such an Enemy at a distance is formidable, while the lurking Serpent lies concealed, and not noticed by the unwary Passenger, darts its fatal Venom. It is necessary then that each Colony should be awake and upon its Guard."

By then, Adams was convinced that independence was the only solution and he was the first prominent leader to express that thought.

When Sam Adams left Boston for Philadelphia in 1774 to represent Massachusetts at the first Continental Congress, his friends presented him with a new outfit and some spending money. The fifty-two-year-old Adams had never before traveled out of the Boston area. His many friends had also chipped in numerous times to fix up his house on Boston Harbor. Although Adams was a failure as a businessman, his morality, integrity, and commitment to the cause of justice were unquestioned and he was much admired by his fellow freedom-loving Bostonians.

"For my own part, I have been wont to converse with poverty," he later wrote. "And however disagreeable she may be thought to be by the affluent and luxurious who never were acquainted with her, I can live happily with her the remainder of my days, if I can thereby contribute to the redemption of my Country."

Adams was born in Boston. His father was a successful brewer, a deacon in the Old South Church and politically active. Adams jumped into politics himself at an early age. Although he initially thought separation from England would be a mistake, he railed against tyranny and "taxation without representation." He was tireless in his writings. He came to hate the British governance and the British officials came to hate him. Adams organized a boycott of British goods and, in 1773, the Boston Tea Party, in which his Sons of Liberty, dressed as Indians, dumped tea from impounded ships into Boston Harbor. When Massachusetts' royal governor Thomas Gage offered pardon to American rebels in 1775 if they laid down their arms, he excluded Samuel Adams and John Hancock.

Gage could not have known how close he came to capturing the patriotic pair—Adams and Hancock were staying in a Lexington tavern on April 18, the night before the battles of Lexington and Concord. Paul Revere was sent on his celebrated "Midnight Ride" to warn them that British troops were on the move.

"I saw two officers on horse-back," Paul Revere later wrote. "I was near enough to see their holsters and cockades. One of them started his horse towards me, the other up the road, as I supposed, to head me, should I escape the first. I turned my horse short about, and rode upon a full gallop for Mistick Road. He followed me about 300 yards, and finding he could not catch me, returned. I proceeded to Lexington, through Mistick, and alarmed Mr. Adams and Col. Hancock."

Adams and Hancock, with Revere's help, left Lexington just hours before the hostilities began. The capture of the two leaders would have been the ultimate prize for the British that day.

During the war, Adams served in the Continental Congress, traveling often between Boston and Philadelphia. He signed the Declaration of Independence. The village of Adams was incorporated in western Massachusetts in 1778 and named after him. He helped write the Massachusetts Constitution with his cousin John Adams and helped draft the Articles of Confederation. He remained eloquent in the cause of freedom.

"If ye love wealth greater than liberty, the tranquility of servitude greater than the animating contest for freedom, go home from us in peace," he wrote to Tories who remained loyal to Britain. "We seek not your counsel, nor your arms. Crouch down and lick the hand that feeds you; May your chains set lightly upon you, and may posterity forget that ye were our countrymen."

Sam Adams's grandfather was an English sea captain who settled near Mount Wollaston, just south of Boston. His father, also Samuel Adams, and his mother had twelve children, but only three survived. They lived in a large home on the waterfront in Boston. Samuel Adams later wrote that his father, who was a Boston selectman, was a "wise and good man." When Sam was a boy, the "Caulkers Club" met at the Adams home; the word eventually evolved to the "caucus" we use today.

In his 1885 book *Samuel Adams*, Hosmer wrote that "all classes were readers" in eighteenth-century Boston. The town's periodicals were filled with letters on political matters signed with pen names, much like the signatures of the citizen-journalists who fill cyberspace with weblogs ("blogs") today. "The five newspapers, the people may be said to have edited themselves," Hosmer wrote.

Samuel Adams's thesis for his master's degree at Harvard in 1743 was entitled "Whether it be lawful to resist the Supreme Magistrate if the Commonwealth cannot otherwise be preserved." He delivered it to an audience that included the royal governor.

Upon graduation, Adams tried law briefly but his family discouraged him. His father gave him one thousand pounds to start a business. He lent half to friends who never repaid him and lost the other half on his own. He then joined his father in the "malt-house" business at the family home on Purchase Street, but the brewery suffered as both father and son were more interested in politics. Young Sam was already writing copiously to the newspapers.

"One can easily see how the business must have been carried on with some slackness," Hosmer wrote, "since the two partners were marked by such characteristics."

Adams's father then lost the family fortune by bad investments. He died when Sam was twenty-six.

Three years later, Adams married Elizabeth Checkley. Five children were born to Samuel and Elizabeth, only two of whom, Samuel Jr., and Hannah, lived to maturity. The first Mrs. Adams died July 25, 1757. "She left two small children," Adams wrote in the family Bible. "God grant they may inherit her graces."

In 1762, at forty years old, Adams married Elizabeth Wells, the twenty-nine-year old daughter of a friend. He called her Betsy and they remained married until Adams died four decades later. At the time of their marriage, he was still not doing well in business and they were always broke. He lost the brewery in 1765 and failed as a tax collector. But unlike slave-owner Jefferson, Adams walked the walk when it came to all men being equal and born with certain unalienable rights. Despite their constant struggles with money, when Sam and Betsy were given a young black slave girl as a gift in 1765, they immediately set her free.

"Samuel Adams's characterization of Benjamin Franklin as being 'a great philosopher but a poor politician' might be paraphrased as applied to himself as being 'a great politician but a very improvident family man,'" wrote Harry C. and Mary W. Green in 1912's *The Pioneer Mothers of America*. "His whole life was practically given up to public affairs, while private interests, business, and family matters were neglected in a way that would have driven a woman less loyal and even-tempered than Elizabeth Adams to bitter complaint, if not open rebellion. Yet always we find her cheerful and sympathetic; always a faithful and loving wife to Samuel Adams and a tender mother to his motherless children. His business might be going to ruin through neglect while he talked politics with his neighbors on the street corners, his leaky roof go unshingled while he made patriots of the workmen of the sail-lofts and shipyards of Boston, but not one word of complaint or fault-finding do we hear from his family."

Although Sam Adams gave his all to patriotic matters, evidence shows he did love his family deeply. In a letter to Betsy in 1778 after running into his son Samuel, who was serving as a physician with the Continental Army, on the road near Palmer, he wrote, "My Children cannot imagine how much Comfort I have in believing they are virtuous." When the younger Samuel died in 1788 from illness contracted during the war—the fourth of his five children to precede him in death—life lost much luster for the aging patriot. As he grew older, he also suffered from a palsy that caused his hands to shake and his voice to quaver. Following the end of the war, Sam Adams ran for the House of Representatives in the first United States Congressional election, but was unsuccessful.

Still he pressed on.

Like many patriots, Adams became more conservative in his later years, especially in matters that threatened the new country he helped build. Although he supported the French Revolution, he did not support a revolution closer to home. In 1786 and 1787, armed farmers in central and western Massachusetts revolted against taxes and farm foreclosures. When Shays' Rebellion was put down, Adams called for hanging the leaders, even though they claimed they were fighting for the same reasons Adams had used to urge them to fight the British.

"Rebellion against a king may be pardoned, or lightly punished, but the man who dares to rebel against the laws of a republic ought to suffer death," Adams responded.

Only two of the Shaysites were hanged. Governor John Hancock—the man paired in 1775 with Sam Adams as unpardonable patriots—pardoned most of them, some as they stood on the gallows.

Adams's seemingly inconsistent call for executions, along with unfair questions about his motivation before and after the Revolution, denied him his rightful place in the pantheon of American patriots.

"Samuel Adams' reputation suffers in the modern era because of the stigma of a particularly unfavorable and unfair biography of the Boston patriot," wrote Thomas R. Eddlem in *The New American* magazine in 2002. "John C. Miller's 1936 *Samuel Adams: Pioneer in Propaganda* remains the most popular biography of Samuel Adams published in the last 100 years, and yet the author generally assumes the worst possible motivations for Adams' actions. The working premises for the book were that Adams sought independence from the very beginning of his ambitious public life and that Samuel died a lonely and unloved man because he was capable of destroying a government but incapable of building up a new government. These claims are flatly untrue."

Eddlem and most other historians now agree that there is no evidence Adams sought independence from Britain before British troops were stationed in Boston in 1768 and that Adams played a huge post-war role in forming the new country. They point to his assisting his cousin in the drafting of the Massachusetts Constitution, which is still in force today, and to his support of the U.S. Constitution and Bill of Rights.

Adams was elected lieutenant governor of Massachusetts in 1789. When Hancock died in 1793, he became governor and was reelected for three one-year terms. He did not seek reelection in 1797. He died in Boston on October 2, 1803.

"He was truly a great man," Thomas Jefferson said, "wise in council, fertile in resources, immovable in his purposes."

5

Daniel Shays, 1747–1825
Reluctant Leader of a Little Rebellion

In the late afternoon of January 25, 1787, more than twelve hundred armed men, many in the blue uniform jackets of the Continental Army, marched through the cold and crusted snow toward the federal arsenal at Springfield.

They were led by Captain Daniel Shays, a thirty-nine-year-old hardscrabble farmer from Pelham who had fought at the Revolutionary War battles of Bunker Hill, Saratoga, and Stony Point. Shays had served his fledgling country so gallantly that the Marquis de Lafayette had even presented him with a sword as a gift.

On this day, though, the men following Shays were facing not the British, but local militia serving under General William Shepard. Five years had passed since George Washington's victory over the British at Yorktown, but the thirteen colonies were still aligned only by the Articles of Confederation and had no national army.

Shays' men—farmers who called themselves regulators or Shaysites—aimed to seize the arsenal, its cannons, ammunition, and firearms. Shays thought, due to a missed communication, that four hundred more insurgents under Luke Day would be joining him from the north and six hundred more under Eli Parsons would be coming from the Berkshires to the west.

Instead, fifty miles to the east, a militia of 4,400 well-armed men under General Benjamin Lincoln was approaching from Worcester. The only hope for Shays' army was to seize the arsenal and its weapons before Lincoln arrived.

When Shays' ragtag troops were 250 yards away from the arsenal, Shays, pistol in one hand and sword in the other, gave the command and the men began moving at double time. When they reached 100 yards, Shepard ordered the arsenal's howitzers fired. The first two shots were aimed over the heads of the regulators. The third was not. The grapeshot killed four men and wounded twenty others. The fourth and fifth shots scattered the farmers, who cried "Murder, murder" as they retreated.

"Sir," Shepard wrote Governor James Bowdoin the next day, "the unhappy time has come when we have been obliged to shed blood. . . . Had I been disposed to destroy them, I might have charged upon their rear and flanks with my infantry and two field pieces and could have killed the greater part of his whole army within 25 minutes."

Shays and his regulators retreated to Chicopee. Lincoln soon arrived at Springfield and sent his cavalry up the frozen Connecticut River to prevent Day and the other insurgents from joining Shays' men. Shays sent a message to Shepard: "Sir, I desire you to send my dead and wounded by my flagg, so that I can burye my dead and take care of my wounded."

"Legend has it that Shays overestimated the number of his dead," wrote Marion L. Starkey in her 1955 book, *A Little Rebellion*, "and that Shepard, snapping out of the unprofessional pity that had nearly mastered him at the time of the attack, retorted that he lacked so many corpses 'but that if Shays would attack the Arsenal again General Shepard would furnish him with as many [dead] rebels as he should desire.'"

Leaving Chicopee in the snow, and pursued by Lincoln and reinforcement troops from New York, Shays and his men made their way back to the hills of Petersham, the central Massachusetts home of Luke Day. There, Lincoln's militia—after a thirty-mile forced march through a blinding blizzard—caught up with them in early February and the regulators scattered, many, including Shays with his wife Abigail, escaping north to Vermont, which had no extradition agreement with Massachusetts.

Shays' Rebellion was effectively over, although small skirmishes continued around New England for more than a month. According to 1829's *A History of the County of Berkshire, Massachusetts,* in late February, eighty insurgents under Captain Perez Hamlin "made an irruption . . . into Stockbridge at midnight, which they pillaged at their pleasure" and took several citizens hostage. Militia ambushed the insurgents in Sheffield the next day. During the fight, two regulators and two militiamen were killed.

Daniel Shays was a reluctant leader, but once involved, he was totally committed. By the time of the assault on the Springfield arsenal he fully expected to die on the gallows. Just four months earlier, he had become the figurehead and last best hope for thousands of subsistence farmers in New England, mostly in western and central Massachusetts.

Inspired by Samuel Adams and others who decried "taxation without representation," Shays and many of the other insurgents had fought the British in the Revolution for little or no pay. Now they were desperate and much of the desperation was due to the Commonwealth's ever-increasing taxes to pay down war debt owed to the mercantile associates of Governor Bowdoin in Boston. Many good men, neighbors of the regulators, were being jailed for nonpayment of taxes and for other debts, and their farms were being foreclosed on.

At first, the farmers, or yeomen as they were called, had attempted to redress their economic problems nonviolently. They met in county conventions modeled on the Committees of Correspondence that had worked so well in New England before the Revolution. Between 1784 and 1787, yeomen in seventy-three rural Massachusetts towns—more than 30 percent of all communities in the state—sent petitions to the legislature in Boston seeking relief from the courts and from the burden of taxes and debts. Farmers in New Hampshire, Vermont, and Connecticut did the same.

"This business must and will progress from one stage to another until it amounts to a pretty formidable rebellion," Henry Knox, secretary of war for the Confederation, wrote in 1786.

Knox was right. In the summer of 1786—before Shays had even joined the movement—many Massachusetts farmers had risen up to close debtors' courts in Northampton and Worcester. In Worcester, they prevented Judge Artemus Ward of Shrewsbury, the first Commander in Chief of the Continental Army, from opening the court with their bayonets pressed to his rotund belly. No blood was shed though. The regulators even listened as Ward lectured them from the courthouse steps for two hours about why what they were doing was wrong.

Shays, born into a Scotch-Irish family in the town of Hopkinton in central Massachusetts, had been poor his entire life. He did not even own his own farm when the Revolution started, but had been a hired hand on a farm in Brookfield. Although initially reluctant to take up arms again, Shays, like his rural neighbors, was desperate. He had long ago sold the sword Lafayette gave him to pay bills. He had also been taken to court for debt, although not jailed, and there he witnessed the bed of a sick woman taken from under her to satisfy a claim.

Captain Shays immediately became a leader of the "rebellion" when he did join, largely because of the respect he had earned in the Revolution. Riding his white horse in September of 1786, he led six hundred regulators in an attempt to close the Springfield court. He was as eager to prevent bloodshed as Shepard, who was charged with stopping him that day. The two men worked out an agreement that allowed the court to open and for the regulators to parade through the streets of Springfield, where many sympathizers joined the march. The court closings continued elsewhere in the state.

In October, the insurgents rejected the Commonwealth's Indemnity Act, which would have pardoned most of them if they renounced closing the courts. On November 30, militia from Boston roughed up the wife and children of farmer and insurgent leader Job Shattuck in Groton, and then tracked Shattuck through freshly fallen snow to the banks of the Nashua River. Shattuck resisted arrest and during the ensuing fight a militiaman wielding a sword severed the cartilage on his leg. Shattuck was then dumped in a jail, and without medical treatment, he became crippled for life.

Within a week, Shays issued a renewed call to arms.

"The seeds of war are now sown; two of our men are now bleeding," a document signed by Shays declared. "I request you to let this letter be read and for you and every man to supply men and provision to relieve us with a reinforcement. . . . We are determined here to carry our point. Our cause is yours. Don't give yourself a rest and let us die here, for we are all brethren."

The lines had been drawn. The regulators—numbering at least three thousand by now—continued to close the courts in Worcester, Hampshire, and Berkshire counties. People in Boston fully expected and prepared for an attack by the insurgents. Merchants donated funds to raise a militia of 4,400 men, a "state of war" was declared, and rumors flew that Shays planned to raid the Bank of Boston to pay his men now gathering in Pelham. Shepard, writing from his home in Westfield, accused Shays of planning "the subversion of the constitution and government at one bold stroke . . . and to erect a military government for the coercion of the state by setting up his own standard . . . to be supported by great numbers from all the states, and be able to declare himself dictator of the whole union."

In a speech on January 12, Governor Bowdoin said he would call on his "full power" to protect the Commonwealth's courts from Shays and his men.

"It is now become apparent that the object of the insurgents is to annihilate our present happy constitution," Bowdoin said.

That was hardly the case, at least in the beginning. The insurgents had issued a press release of sorts after closing the court in Worcester the previous summer. Their actions had not been designed, "as has injuriously been reported, to subvert all government and throw all things into a state of anarchy and confusion," but "to relieve the distresses of . . . fellow citizens until redress of grievances . . . could be obtained in the General Court [the Massachusetts Legislature]. . . . We sincerely deprecate the consequences of anarchy, and we regret to transact anything contrary to the laws of the Commonwealth, but . . . we are induced by the ties of friendship and by, as we trust, the stronger laws which religion inculcates, of doing as we would be done by."

The greatest desire of Shays and his men trudging through the snow in January remained righting the wrongs they saw being committed upon their neighbors. They had twice rejected pardons, and as they marched toward Springfield, they opened jails and released farmers like themselves who had been imprisoned.

Many of the farmers in the jail and in the regulator columns, Shays included, had returned from the Revolution without any pay in their pockets, except for promissory notes that Boston speculators, including many associates of Bowdoin, soon snapped up from them at a fraction of their face value.

By the mid-1780s, the farmers in central and western Massachusetts were broke and desperate. Before the war, they had raised only what their families needed and bartered for the little they could not raise. After the war, they had been thrust into a market economy, and eastern merchants wanted hard currency for goods the farmers had purchased on credit. Massachusetts had fallen into a general depression and, on top of that, farmers were also being ordered by the Commonwealth to pay even more taxes than they had paid to the British—all so the governor's friends who had snapped up the notes could be paid full value for them. The Commonwealth was demanding silver or gold, but there was little silver or gold to be had.

Without paper money in circulation, the farmers had no way to move their surplus crops and their debts continued to mount. Land that had been cleared by their own hands, land that they had fought to free from British rule and taxation, was foreclosed on and farmers were being imprisoned. Many of those same farmers had responded heroically to the call to arms in 1775—Massachusetts had supplied 25 percent of the Continental Army's soldiers—and now Boston was jailing them and taking their farms.

By 1786, men like Daniel Shays had had enough.

"We have lately emerged from a bloody war in which liberty was the glorious prize aimed at," wrote Adam Wheeler of Hubbardston, the leader of the first Worcester court closing, who had been a captain during the Revolution and who had also previously served in the French and Indian War. "I earnestly stepped forth in defense of this country, and cheerfully fought to gain this prize, and liberty is still the object I have in view."

Shays' Rebellion was in many ways a class war. Some of the poor and desperate farmers marching on the Springfield arsenal that day did not even carry muskets—they carried clubs or pitchforks instead. They had no uniforms except for the coats and hats they had worn as Revolutionary soldiers. Instead, the veterans and the teens who had joined them wore sprigs of hemlock in their hats so they could identify one another.

"A few historians have interpreted this confrontation as a class conflict in purely economic terms," wrote David P. Szatmary in his 1980 book *Shays' Rebellion: The Making of an Agrarian Insurrection*. "Such a position, however, may be misleading. Undeniably, the rebellion became primarily a contest between two economic classes: yeomen who faced the loss of their properties, and merchants, lawyers and speculators who stood to gain from these losses. But without neglecting the economic base of the turmoil, it seems clear that Shays' Rebellion can be more fully understood as an economic conflict exacerbated by a cultural clash between a commercial society and a rural, subsistence-oriented way of life."

Marker in field in Sheffield, Massachusetts

To many in New England, Shays became a folk hero. To the merchants and wealthy establishment, though, he was a great threat to the shaky future of the former colonies. "I am mortified beyond expression," George Washington, retired on his farm in Virginia, wrote a friend, "when I view the clouds that have spread over the brightest morn that ever dawned upon any country."

Gore Vidal, in his 2003 *Inventing a Nation*, wrote the "the rhetoric of the Shaysites was calculated to terrify the merchant class" because the farmers spoke about "common property."

"In this crisis there were no Federalists, no future Republicans, only frightened men of property," Vidal wrote. "Most, by now, wanted to create a strong new nation where no revolt like that of Daniel Shays could ever happen again and where tranquility, if not happiness, was the common pursuit."

Although few were killed in the short-lived rebellion, it has been called America's first civil war. In the Berkshires of western Massachusetts, a judge named William Whiting sided with Shays' insurgents.

"When he wasn't sitting on the bench," Starkey wrote, "[Whiting] rode about the county with his medicine bags as country doctor. In that capacity he had perhaps closer acquaintance with the miseries of the people than most judges, and he was all for them. 'I have never heard anybody point out a better way to have their grievances redressed than the people have taken,' he was saying. 'If the law had gone on two years longer in the way it has done, the common people would all be slaves . . . it is the indispensable duty of the people at large in all free republican governments to guard their liberties.'"

Debate over the fate of the insurgents—two hundred were indicted—dominated the Commonwealth and the other fledgling states in the early months of 1787. Sam Adams, of all people, called for hangings.

"Rebellion against a king may be pardoned, or lightly punished, but the man who dares to rebel against the laws of a republic ought to suffer death," the great patriot wrote.

Thomas Jefferson, writing from France, disagreed: "A little rebellion now and then is a good thing," Jefferson said. "It is a medicine necessary for the sound health of government. God forbid that we should ever be 20 years without such a rebellion."

In the summer of 1787, newly elected governor John Hancock pardoned most of the offenders, even the leaders. Some insurgents, as a face-saving measure for the authorities, were paraded dramatically to the gallows before they received their reprieves in June. Two insurgents were hanged, but their charges included burglary.

Shays, who was pardoned in 1788, returned briefly to Pelham from Vermont, couldn't make a living, and moved to a town called Sparta in upstate New York.

"Sometimes travelers came to look him up, exactly as wayfarers in Virginia stopped off at Mount Vernon for a look at its celebrated squire," Starkey wrote. "One of them, a future President of the United States, young Millard Fillmore, was disappointed in what he found. Shays had become an old man like any other, a bit too fond of the bottle, they said in Sparta, but not one to frequent low places or keep low company. In spite of his slender means, he set a good table and entertained graciously. But there was nothing about him to suggest the legendary figure that had caused the hills of Berkshire to ring with the cry 'Hurrah for Daniel Shays!'"

Shays died in 1825 and was buried in an unmarked grave. Sparta later became Cornish, New York. Shays is memorialized by the Daniel Shays Highway, built in 1935 through western Massachusetts, and by monuments erected in Springfield and Pelham. Both a rock band in California and a Celtic band in Massachusetts have called themselves Shays' Rebellion.

The greatest legacy of Shays' Rebellion, however, is that it helped shape the federal Constitution and then spurred the adoption of the Bill of Rights.

When Constitutional Convention delegates met in Philadelphia in May 1787, Shays' Rebellion was fresh in their minds, so they constructed a national government with the power to directly raise taxes, maintain a national army, call up the state militia in time of national emergency, and still guarantee each state a republican form of government. George Washington said the insurrection was the reason he appeared at the convention as, "there could be no stronger evidence of the want of energy in our governments than these disorders."

On February 6, 1788, Massachusetts became the sixth state to ratify the Constitution despite strong opposition in central and western counties. The Massachusetts backers of the Constitution finally won the vote for "conditional ratification" by promising to promote a series of amendments protecting individual liberties—laying the basis for the first ten amendments in the Bill of Rights.

6

Isaiah Thomas, 1749–1831
The Patriotic Ink-Stained Wretch

Isaiah Thomas was just six years old when his ne'er-do-well father abandoned his family in 1756. His already destitute mother had four older children and couldn't provide for Isaiah too, so the Overseers of the Poor of the Town of Boston indentured him to a childless printer named Zechariah Fowle.

Little Isaiah was soon standing on a crate in Fowle's shop setting cold type, an auspicious start to the career of America's greatest printer.

Fowle and his partner Samuel Draper taught young Isaiah everything they knew about printing. By the time he was sixteen, Thomas was virtually running the shop, a fortunate twist of fate for freedom-loving Americans a decade later. If Samuel Adams was the propagandist of the American Revolution, Isaiah Thomas was its reporter and printer. He even got the scoop on the battles of Lexington and Concord. Thomas's eyewitness accounts of the April 19, 1775 skirmishes in his *The Massachusetts Spy, or, American Oracle of Liberty* are believed to be the first published anywhere.

"Americans! Forever bear in mind the BATTLE of LEXINGTON!" Thomas wrote. "Where British Troops, unmolested and unprovoked, wantonly, and in a most inhumane manner, fired upon and killed a number of our countrymen,

Isaiah Thomas

then robbed them of their provisions, ransacked, plundered and burnt their houses! Nor could the cries of defenseless women, some of whom were in the pains of childbirth, the cries of helpless babes, nor the prayers of old age, confined to beds of sickness, appease their thirst for blood!—or divert them from their DESIGN of MURDER and ROBBERY!"

Thomas was just twenty-five years old then, but already a seasoned newspaperman and an unapologetic patriot. Nine years earlier, he had a falling out with Fowle, left Boston, and headed for London where he hoped to further his craft. He never made it beyond Nova Scotia, where he worked for printer Anthony Henry and his *Halifax Gazette*. In 1765, the British imposed the Stamp Act tax on businesses in the colonies, including Nova Scotia. Thomas put a paragraph on the front page of the *Gazette* that said Nova Scotians were "disgusted."

In his 1810 book, *The History of Printing in America*, Thomas recalled being a scared seventeen-year-old summoned before the British secretary of the province. "'How dare you publish in the *Gazette* that the people of Nova Scotia are displeased with the Stamp Act?' the secretary demanded. 'I thought it was true,' Thomas answered."

Thomas then left Nova Scotia for Charleston, South Carolina, where he worked again as a printer. In 1770, he returned to Boston with a determination to produce the colonies' greatest newspaper and with a new wife, Mary Dill.

"The connection was not a happy one," according to their grandson, Benjamin Franklin Thomas. In 1777, Isaiah Thomas divorced Dill after discovering her affair with Benjamin Thompson—a loyalist. Two years later he married Mary Thomas Fowle, a widow. She had two daughters by her earlier marriage and she also raised Thomas's two children from his marriage to Dill.

"As the head of a family, she was faithful to the charge committed to her, and endeavored with scrupulous exactness to perform her duty towards those over whom she was called to exercise her protection and care," Thomas wrote in her obituary in 1818. "Her heart always melted to the tale of woe, and her hand was never slow to follow its sacred impulse."

In a memoir about his grandfather published in 1874, Benjamin Franklin Thomas described Isaiah Thomas as, "tall and handsome in person." Others described him as homely. Pulitzer Prize winner Esther Forbes in her book *Paul Revere and the World He Lived In* wrote Thomas possessed "an ugly, smart, one-sided face, eyes bright as buttons under rough black brows, and a heavy full mouth." Regardless of whether Thomas had a newspaper face, no one disputes his patriotism or his ability as a printer.

Back in Boston, he began publishing the *Massachusetts Spy, or Thomas's Boston Journal.* His old mentor, Zechariah Fowle, was briefly his partner before retiring. As was the custom of the day, many of the columns in the *Spy* were essays by citizens, often signed with pen names. Thomas, in his *History of Printing,* described his own publishing efforts in the third person.

> For a few weeks some communications were furnished by those who were in favor of the royal prerogative, but they were exceeded by the writers on the other side; and the authors and subscribers among the Tories denounced and quitted the Spy. The publisher then devoted it to the cause of his country, supported by the Whigs, under whose banners he had enlisted. Writers of various classes, in the Whig interest, furnished essays, which in a very considerable degree aided in preparing the public mind for events which followed. Common sense in common language is necessary to influence one class of citizens, as much as learning and elegance of composition are to produce an effect upon another. The cause of America was just, and it was only necessary to state this cause in a clear and impressive manner, to unite the American people in its support.

No one doubted which side Thomas took—two weeks before the Revolution began, John Hancock sent a letter from the Provincial Congress at Concord with the salutation: "To Mr. Isaiah Thomas, Supporter of the Rights and Liberties of Mankind." The Sons of Liberty often met at the *Spy* office. The newspaper infuriated British officials—"The *Spy* had among its contributors several able and pungent writers who did not put on their gloves when they wrote," Thomas's grandson said. In 1771, irate royal governor Thomas Hutchinson ordered that Thomas be prosecuted for malicious libel, but a grand jury refused to indict him. Loyalists in North Carolina burned the Boston publisher in effigy, which made Thomas proud. British soldiers also tried to intimidate Thomas. In March 1775, a man who had been tarred and feathered was paraded through the Boston streets by a regiment of Red Coats. "The regiment, with the colonel at its head, halted before the *Spy* office," Thomas later wrote, "the music playing the Rogue's March, some of the soldiers vociferating 'the printer of the *Spy* shall be the next to receive this punishment.'"

The stationing of British troops in Boston had particularly angered Thomas, as well as Sam Adams and other Boston patriots.

"On the 7th of July, 1774 . . . just after the landing of four additional regiments of troops, with a train of royal artillery, a new political device appeared in the title of this paper—a snake and a dragon," Thomas later wrote in his *History of Printing*. "The dragon represented Great Britain, and the snake the colonies. The snake was divided into nine parts . . . . Over the several parts of the snake was this motto, in large capitals, 'JOIN OR DIE!' This device, which was extended under the whole width of the title of the *Spy*, appeared in every succeeding paper whilst it was printed in Boston. Its publication ceased in that town on the 6th of April, 1775, and on the 19th of that month hostilities between Great Britain and America commenced. A few days before this event took place, its publisher sent, privately, a press and types to Worcester . . . it was now *The Massachusetts Spy, or, American Oracle of Liberty*; headed with 'Americans! Liberty or Death! Join or Die!'"

Thomas barely made it out of Boston in time. At the urging of friends and fellow patriots, he sent his press to Worcester, forty miles inland, on a wagon on April 16. Worcester was a safe haven for the young publisher; once a Loyalist stronghold the town became a hotbed of patriotism and the British never attacked it during the war. On the morning of April 19, "[I] crossed from Boston over to Charlestown in a boat with Dr. Joseph Warren, went to Lexington, and joined the provincial militia in opposing the king's troops," Thomas wrote. He rode into Worcester on a borrowed horse the next day. His press and equipment rolled into town two days later and he went to work. The flat bed screw press, the same one Thomas had learned on as a boy, required handset type and each sheet had to be impressed and pulled off manually. It is now preserved at the American Antiquarian Society, which Thomas founded years later.

Thomas based his stories of the battles of Lexington and Concord on what he saw and what other eyewitnesses told him. Here he describes the first skirmish in Lexington:

The body of the [British] troops in the meantime, under the command of Lt. Colonel Smith, had crossed the river and landed at Phipps's farm; they immediately to the number of 2,000 proceeded to Lexington, six miles below Concord, with great silence. A company of militia, of about 80 men, mustered near the meeting-house; the troops came in sight of them just before sunrise; the militia upon seeing the troops began to disperse; the troops then set out upon the run, hallooing and huzzaing, and coming within a few rods of them, the commanding officer accosted the militia in words to this effect, "Disperse you damned rebels!—Damn you, disperse!" Upon which the troops again huzzaed, and immediately one or two officers discharged their pistols, which were instantaneously followed by the firing of four or five soldiers, and then there seemed a general discharge from the whole body; it is to be noticed that they fired upon our people as they were dispersing, agreeable to their command, and that we did not even return the fire: eight of our men were killed and nine wounded;—the troops then laughed and damned the Yankees, and said they could not bear the smell of gun powder. . . .

Then Thomas described the battle at Concord:

Thus did the troops of Britain's king fire FIRST at two several times upon his loyal American subjects, and put a period to ten lives before one gun was fired at them. . . . Our people THEN returned the fire and obliged the troops to retreat . . . back to Lexington, both provincials and troops firing as they went . . . just as the retreating party had got there they made a stand, picked up their dead and took all the carriages they could find and put their wounded thereon; others of them to their eternal disgrace be it spoken, were robbing and setting houses on fire and discharging their cannon at the meeting house.

Hardly objective journalism—for example, the British set the houses on fire because Minutemen arriving on the scene from around the countryside were using them as cover while they fired upon the retreating army. Thomas's account, however, was no more biased than the report that appeared in the *London Gazette* on June 10 that accused the Americans of "cruelty and barbarity," including scalping and cutting the ears off of wounded British troops.

Thomas continued to publish his *Massachusetts Spy* whenever possible throughout the Revolution, although the war disrupted the economy, subscriptions dropped precipitously, and Thomas had to contend with poor ink, worn-out type and shortages of paper. He even put an ad in the *Spy* in 1780 that read, "It is earnestly requested that the fair Daughters of Liberty . . . would not neglect to serve their country, by saving for the Paper-Mill, all Linen and Cotton and Linen Rags, be they ever so small, as they are equally good for the purpose of making paper . . . if the Ladies should not make a fortune by this piece of economy, they will at least have the satisfaction of knowing they are doing an essential service to the community."

Despite all obstacles, Thomas persevered. He chronicled—and probably organized—Worcester's celebration of Independence Day, the first in the nation, on July 4, 1779. "The Sons of Freedom presided over the ringing of bells, the firing of cannons and a display of the Continental flag," the *Spy* reported. "At 12 o'clock 13 cannons were fired. In the evening the Court House was illuminated and a display of other fireworks greatly to the satisfaction of many respectable and staunch friends to the common cause of our nation."

Thomas earlier had given the first public reading in Massachusetts of the Declaration of Independence. In addition to being a publisher, Thomas was also postmaster of Worcester and he had intercepted a post rider heading for Boston from Philadelphia with the Declaration less than three weeks after Thomas Jefferson finished writing it. Only John Hancock had signed it then; the other signers added their signatures in August. On July 24, 1776, Thomas read the Declaration to a wildly cheering crowd from the balcony of the South Church next to the Worcester Common. "He may well have had a just pride in the reading of that Declaration," his grandson wrote. "He could not fail to see it was grounded on principles he had been among the earliest to espouse and defend."

After the war, Thomas prospered as a printer and bookseller. He owned a printing house in Worcester and another in Boston. He produced more than nine hundred books, including one hundred titles for children. His company operated sixteen presses and printed textbooks, bibles, songbooks, and many other publications. His *Massachusetts Magazine* failed but *Thomas' New England Almanac* thrived nationally and brought in regular profits. The almanac included astronomical data, plus poems, jokes, political essays, and pages for daily records and expenses. Fellow printer and patriot Benjamin Franklin called Thomas the "Baskerville of America," referencing John Baskerville, an English printer of the eighteenth century, renowned for his innovative type design and beautiful books.

Thomas also owned bookstores in Massachusetts, New Hampshire, New York, and Maryland. He continued to publish the *Spy* but, ever the businessman, changed the name to *Worcester Magazine* from 1786 to 1788 to avoid a state tax on advertisements placed in newspapers.

"[Thomas] reduced the size from folio to octavo, and then continued the same kind of news that he had published in his newspaper," historian Clarence Brigham wrote. "When the state lifted the tax, he resumed in newspaper form."

When the *Spy* was restored in April of 1788, it had a new motto taken from the new Massachusetts Constitution: "The Liberty of the Press is essential to the security of freedom."

In 1801, Thomas turned over the publishing of the *Spy* and his other business interests to his only son, Isaiah Thomas Jr., and began research for his book, *The History of Printing in America*. He published the first edition in two volumes in 1810. It is still regarded as the most trusted source of information on printing in this country between 1640 and 1800.

In 1812, Thomas established the American Antiquarian Society dedicated to preserving the "literature of liberty"—newspapers, broadsides, books, pamphlets, letters, and other periodicals. He donated money and his private library, which included eight thousand books. He personally visited newspaper offices and purchased back issues. The Society's library in Worcester contains nearly three million books, pamphlets, broadsides, manuscripts, prints, and maps, and more than three million copies of American newspapers printed before 1877. The collection is one-third larger than that of the Library of Congress.

After Mary's death in 1818, Thomas married Rebecca Armstrong, but separated from her three years later. In 1819, Isaiah Thomas Jr., died from injuries suffered in a fall at age forty-five. The younger Thomas left nine children. Isaiah Thomas Sr. particularly cherished a portrait his son had sat for a year earlier—the painting hung in Isaiah Sr.'s bedroom in

Worcester until his own death on April 4, 1831. Now portraits of father and son, as well as their wives, hang together in the American Antiquarian Society library.

In 1845, the flourishing *Spy,* which Isaiah Thomas Jr. had moved back to Boston in 1810, went from weekly to daily publication. It continued to be published by other owners until 1904.

7

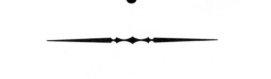

The Official Heroine of the
Commonwealth Fought Like a Man

The Revolutionary War continued long after Cornwallis's surrender at Yorktown in October 1781. Though Yorktown was the last major battle in the War for American Independence, British soldiers still held New York City for two years, and bands of Loyalists, with the aid of Indian allies, fought on elsewhere. The Treaty of Paris officially ending the war would not be signed until September 1783.

Many of the men who fought on the side of liberty, however, some for more than six years, had had enough by Yorktown. They had seldom been paid, if at all, and longed to return to their farms and pre-war lives. Some deserted from the Continental Army and others refused re-enlistment.

Into the void stepped eighteen-year-old Robert Shurtliff. Seven months after Yorktown, the slender but muscular Shurtliff enlisted with the Massachusetts Fourth Regiment in Uxbridge as a "three-year man." Shurtliff served for the next seventeen months. During that time he was wounded twice, found out to be a woman, served several more months, and was honorably discharged.

Found out to be a woman?

DEBORAH SAMPSON.

Published by H. Mann. 1797.

Rendering in Herman Mann's biography

That's right. Robert Shurtliff was actually Deborah Samson, who had traveled forty-five miles from her home in Middleborough to Worcester County so no one would recognize her when she enlisted disguised as a man. For the next year and a half she bound up her small breasts, bathed privately in rivers, avoided the latrines, and fought valiantly in skirmishes in New York. She even tried to tend to her own wound to avoid discovery and suffered for the rest of her life because of her clumsy attempt to remove a musket ball lodged in her thigh. She was finally found out when she contracted a fever and became delirious. An army doctor tore away her upper garments to treat her, and discovered not the chest of Robert Shurtliff, but the breasts of Deborah Samson.

Samson, more often but erroneously spelled Sampson, was born poor in Plympton, a small farming town inland from Plymouth.

"Setting the scraps of her biography in what we can piece together about the different worlds she entered gives us a story of a remarkable transformation," Alfred Young wrote in *Masquerade: The Life and Times of Deborah Sampson, Continental Soldier* in 2004. "To use [early biographer Herman] Mann's words, she was a 'young female of low birth and station' who rebelled against "a contracted female sphere.'"

Samson's mother, Deborah Bradford Samson, was the great-granddaughter of William Bradford, the early Plymouth Colony governor. Samson's father, Jonathan Samson, was also a descendent of a family that came to America on the Mayflower. By the time Deborah and her seven siblings had arrived, however, the family had hit the skids. Deborah's father and mother fought constantly and when she was five years old, her father left. For years, legend had it that he went to sea and died in a shipwreck, but Jonathan Samson had actually abandoned his wife and children and wound up in Maine with another woman.

Samson's mother had no way to support her children. Deborah was sent to live first with relatives and then with strangers over the next five years. "As I was born to be unfortunate, my sun soon clouded," she told Mann years later.

At ten years old, Deborah became an indentured servant on Jeremiah Thomas's farm in nearby Middleborough. She worked hard, taught herself to read, and then read voraciously. She became a rebellious young woman and left the Congregational Church to join the less-accepted Baptists. She was fifteen when the Revolution started and was horrified by the reports of violence that came out of the battles of Lexington and Concord. Even though she had never been to school herself, at eighteen years old she became a schoolteacher for a couple of years. She supplemented her teacher's pay by weaving at homes and at Sproat's Tavern, where men talked about the war and the exploits of local soldiers. She was smitten with patriotism.

"Confirmed by this time in the justness of a defensive war," she said years later, "I only seemed to want the license to become one of the severest avengers of the wrong."

She almost certainly first dressed as a man and signed a male name, Timothy Thayer of Carver, to an enlistment sheet in Middleborough one night. But Timothy Thayer failed to appear at muster the next day and Samson was suspected. She denied she had been the signer but was still chastised by her Baptist minister.

It appears to have been a test run, because she then disguised herself as a man and went to Uxbridge to sign up in a tavern on May 20, 1782. The Continental Army was desperate for recruits and even paid a sixty-pound bounty to anyone who would sign on as a three-year man. No verification of birth was needed. The only qualifications were a man had to be 5-foot-3 or taller and had to have at least two opposing teeth, since the ends of paper charges had to be bitten off during battle. Deborah was at least 5-foot-7, taller than the average man in colonial New England.

Some theorize she joined to escape her life in Middleborough. Others suggest she craved adventure. She claimed to have been motivated by pure patriotism.

"Take the big question of 'why did she do it?'—that is, why did she disguise herself and go into the army?" Young told an interviewer after his book was published. "She was a rural woman of the laboring classes, daughter of a farm laborer, an indentured servant, a near orphan more or less abandoned by her family. Her only real option was to become someone's wife and the mother of seven or eight children. But she was unusually gifted and self-educated in book learning—which opened a wider world to her—and she had a wide range of interests. She wanted something more out of life."

Before she made the journey to Worcester County, she cut her long blonde hair off. Deborah had a jutting, man-like chin and a prominent nose and, even though she was really twenty-one or twenty-two, she told the recruiters that she was eighteen, probably to explain why Robert Shurtliff didn't have to shave. Her gender was not questioned in Uxbridge and three days later, on May 23, 1782, she was mustered into the Massachusetts 4th Light Infantry in Worcester. The new soldier immediately marched west with her comrades to Westchester County in New York state, an area where confrontations with troops from British-controlled Manhattan still occurred frequently.

The other soldiers in the 4th were soon calling her "Molly" because of her hairless face, blue eyes, and feminine features. None knew the truth though, because "Robert" never loosened her tongue with drink during her time in the service and never put herself in a position, such as in the barracks latrine, where her comrades could discover her gender.

And she fought like a man. Her unit was assigned to protect West Point, a key position that traitor Benedict Arnold had a year earlier tried to convey to the British. The 4th frequently skirmished with Loyalists and their Indian allies. Mann claimed years later that Samson had killed an Indian charging at her with raised tomahawk with a single shot, an account she did not dispute. According to Mann, at least one woman fell in love with blond and blue-eyed "Robert" while she was in the service.

Samson was struck on the head by a saber and shot in the right thigh when Loyalist cavalry ambushed her patrol near Tarrytown, New York. The American soldiers all would have died in the ensuing battle but the Loyalists were driven off by troops serving under Colonel Ebenezer Sproat, the son of the Middleborough tavern owner. Colonel Sproat reportedly did not recognize Samson because she was covered with her own blood.

A French doctor serving with the Continental Army treated the wound on her head but Samson didn't tell him about the musket ball in her thigh. She snuck off and attempted to remove it herself; some accounts say she failed and the ball remained lodged in her leg. Either way, the wound caused her constant pain for years.

In the spring of 1783, the still recovering Samson was serving as a waiter to General John Paterson when her unit was assigned to Philadelphia, according to some accounts to protect the Continental Congress from soldiers who were rioting because they had not been paid. Many soldiers in the 4th contracted a fever while there, Samson among them. Private "Robert Shurtliff" became delirious and when Dr. Barnabus Binney ripped off his shirt to test his heartbeat, he discovered the truth. Deborah begged Dr. Binney to not reveal her secret and he didn't for a time. She continued to serve as a waiter to Paterson for months. Finally, Binney or someone else revealed her gender and she was honorably discharged at West Point on October 23, 1783, one month after the Treaty of Paris was signed.

Samson quietly returned to Massachusetts. Then a front-page story without a headline appeared in the *New York Gazette* on January 10, 1784. It read:

> *An extraordinary instance of virtue in a female soldier, has occurred lately in the American Army, in the Massachusetts line viz, a lively comely young nymph, 19 years old, dressed in man's apparel has been discovered; and what redounds to her honor, she has served in*

the character of a soldier for near three years undiscovered
which time she displayed herself with activity, alertness, ch
and valour, having been in several skirmishes with the enemy
receiving two wounds, a small shot remains in her to this day;
was a remarkably vigilant solider on her post, and always gain
the admiration and applause of her officers; was never found i
liquor; and always kept company with the most upright and tem-
perate soldiers.

For several month this galantress served with credit as a
waiter in a General officer's family; a violent illness (when the
troops were in Philadelphia) led to the discovery of her sex; she has
since been honorably discharged from the army with a reward; and
sent to her connecxions who it appears live Eastward of Boston at a
place called Munduncook.

The cause of her personating a man it is said, proceeded
from the rigour of her parents, who exercised their perogative, to
induce her marriage with a young man she had conceived a great
antipathy for; together with her being a remarkable heroine; and
being warmly attached to her country, in the service of which, it
must be acknowledged, she gained reputation; and no doubt will
be noticed by the compilers of the history of our grand revolution.
She passed by the name of Robert Shurtlieff while in the army,
and was borne on the roles of the regiment as such. For particular
reasons, her real name is withheld, but the facts aforementioned are
unquestionable and unembellished.

Young notes that the facts were indeed embellished. She
was at least twenty-one when she enlisted. She only served seventeen months and she was not escaping from the "rigours" of
her parents because her father had long ago died and she had
little contact with her mother by the time she signed on.

"The article was probably written by one of her senior officers but the information could only have come from her," Young
wrote. "The most likely author was General John Paterson."

The article was reprinted in Boston papers, but it was
only after she married farmer Benjamin Gannett on April 17,

story revealed her name. By then,
d in Sharon, twenty miles outside
ᵥe birth to three children, Earl in
atience in 1790. She and Benjamin
ᵣl, Susanna Baker Shepard, in 1796.
d just forty-nine acres and they lived
January 20, 1792, the Massachusetts
to pay her thirty-four pounds for her
she had not been paid anything during the
ᵤation, signed by Governor John Hancock,
exhibited an extraordinary instance of female
ᵤischarging the duties of a faithful, gallant soldier,
same time preserving the virtue and chastity of her
ᵤspected and unblemished."

The Gannetts still lived in poverty though. In 1797, Debo-
agreed to do an as-told-to book with Mann, a young editor
ᵣom Dedham. In 1802, she became the first woman in America to undertake a paid lecture tour. Writing in the anthology
Women Public Speakers in the United States, 1800 to 1925, Jane
Elmes-Crahall said Samson had two motivations for the tour.
The first was to make money and the second was to prove to a
growing legion of doubters that her story was true.

Dressed in her Continental Army uniform, Samson
performed the same schtick every night—telling her tale in
a speech she and Mann wrote together, loading her musket,
"Old Betsy," and pretending to fire it, and reciting poetry.

Mann's book, *The Female Review; Or, Memoirs of An
American Lady,* is generally considered unreliable. He quotes
Samson throughout, however, and she apparently approved of
Mann's embellishments and did not object to the book's con-
tent. She also did not object when Mann changed the spelling of her maiden name to Sampson. That spelling was used
throughout her "The American Heroine" tour and survives
today. Mann crafted a second version of the book in 1830, three
years after Samson's death. In the first version, Mann had Samson involved in a chaste friendship with a "Miss P." while in

Philadelphia. In the second version, Mann turned it into a steamy lesbian affair.

"The terrible Herman Mann, Sampson's biographer, drove me up the wall on matters of sexuality," Young said in an interview in 2005. "I concluded early on that he simply could not be trusted because he—with Sampson as likely collaborator—made up too much, for example, portraying Sampson at the battle of Yorktown when even he admitted she enlisted the following May. But what to do with Mann's allegations about sexuality . . . or that hearsay in her neighborhood had it that she denied her husband 'the rites of the marriage bed,' possibly because she stopped having children after she had three."

Samson kept a diary while on her tour, which took her to at least twenty communities in the Northeast, including Boston, Worcester, and Albany, but she wrote little about her life as a soldier and as a man. Most of the diary concerns the business of the tour because she handled everything herself, including promotions and finances. Men and women paid twenty-five cents to attend her lectures, and children were admitted at half price.

The best answer to the question "Why did she decide to serve as a man?" lies in what Deborah Samson allegedly told Mann, or at least tacitly approved for his book, and in the handwritten script that she and Mann crafted. She memorized and repeated the script night after night on her tour.

"What particular inducement could she have thus to elope from the soft sphere of her own sex, to perform a deed of valor by way of sacrilege on unhallowed ground—voluntarily to face the storms of both elements and war, in the character of him, who is more fitly made to brave and endure all danger?" she would ask rhetorically.

Then she would answer her own question.

"Wrought upon at length, you may say, by an enthusiasm and phrenzy, that could brook no control—I burst the tyrant bands, which *held my sex in awe*, and clandestinely, or by stealth, grasped an opportunity, which custom and the world seemed to deny, as a natural privilege."

Even with the money from her tour—cut short because she missed her children—the Gannetts lived in poverty. That bothered the great patriot Paul Revere, by then a successful coppersmith who lived in Canton, the town next to Sharon. Revere advocated that Samson should receive the same federal pension that male veterans received and wrote a letter on her behalf to Massachusetts congressman William Eustis in 1804.

"Her husband is a good sort of man, though of small force in business," Revere wrote. "They have a few acres of poor land, which they cultivate, but they are really poor. She told me, she had no doubt that her ill health is in consequence of her being exposed when She did a Soldier's duty."

Samson received her $4 per month pension, the first woman warrior in America to do so. It was later increased to $8 a month in 1819.

The Gannett family fortune improved in Deborah's later years. Her son Earl became a captain in the militia, and he and his wife Mary built a mansion in Sharon. Deborah spent her final years there. She died in the house, which still stands at 300 East Street, on April 29, 1827. She was buried in the nearby Rock Ridge Cemetery, where a grandson later erected a monument to her and to Civil War veterans.

Benjamin survived his wife by eleven years. Just weeks before he died, Congress voted to make him the only man to receive a pension as the widower of a Revolutionary War veteran.

In 1983, Massachusetts governor Michael Dukakis declared Deborah Sampson "Official Heroine of the Commonwealth." Deborah Sampson Gannett Day is celebrated but little noted in Massachusetts on May 23, the day she was mustered into the Continental Army.

8

William Miller, 1782–1849
The Great Disappointer

October 22, 1844 turned out to be a very bad day for a lot of people.

"We looked for our coming Lord until the clock tolled 12 at midnight," farmer Hiram Edson of Port Gibson, New York, wrote. "The day had then passed and our disappointment became a certainty. . . . We wept and wept till the day dawned."

Edson was one of at least fifty thousand people in the United States, mostly in New England and New York, who fully expected and hoped—based on the prediction of William Miller—that they would be lifted into heaven on that day as the world ended in fire.

Throughout the Northeast, tens of thousands who followed Miller waited for the Second Coming of Christ, some donning white ascension robes and climbing hilltops or into trees to be closer to heaven. Some had given away their farms, homes, and all of their worldly possessions. Some committed suicide after the day that forever came to be known as the Great Disappointment passed and their embarrassment became too much to bear.

For her 1924 book, *Days of Delusion*, historian Clara Endicott Sears solicited recollections of the Great Disappointment. Ellen Davenport of Worcester relayed this story from her father, who in 1844 was twenty-five and living in Portland, Maine.

"A great company of men and women made their ascension robes and marched singing through the streets to the Eastern Cemetery, where they believed the dead were to rise," Davenport told Sears. "One man kneeled on his first wife's grave, saying, 'Here I will stay till I meet my beloved, and ascend with her;' which so incensed his second wife that she refused ever to live with him again."

Miller, a pudgy, mild-mannered sixty-two-year-old preacher, had originally predicted God would "purify the earth by fire causing the wicked and all their works to be consumed in the general conflagration" sometime during the year preceding March 21, 1844. It didn't happen. March 22, 1844 dawned as usual. Six months later, however, one of Miller's followers recalculated the date to include "tarrying time," and the new doomsday, October 22, was eagerly accepted, especially after Miller wholeheartedly endorsed it.

"Crops were left unharvested, their owners expecting never to want what they had raised," Luther Boutelle, a Millerite preacher from Groton, wrote in his memoirs. "Men paid up their debts. Many sold their property to help others to pay their debts. . . . Beef cattle were slaughtered and distributed among the poor."

In *Days of Delusion,* Sears called Groton and the rest of north-central Massachusetts, "the very heart of what was once one of the most vital rural centres of the great excitement in 1843–44." Western New York's "Burned-Over District"—so called because so much nineteenth-century revivalist activity occurred there—was another. Boston was the urban center. In the four years leading up to the Great Disappointment, Joshua V. Himes, a younger Millerite preacher from the Hub, led a media blitz that produced books, tracts, and newspapers at a staggering rate. Those printed pieces, estimated at one for every five persons in the United States, all had one message— repent, the end is at hand. The words of "Prophet Miller" and other Millerite preachers who fanned out as far as Ohio and Washington, D.C.—at least twenty of whom were female—whipped people into a frenzy. No believer wanted to be left behind in the burning world that Miller envisioned.

"Bodies of human beings were underneath the ruins in every place, some dashed in pieces, some without heads, and some whose limbs were severed from their trunks, and in every form that death could prey upon the human frame," Miller wrote, describing the scene from the viewpoint of a left-behind sinner. "Some, still in life, though wounded, filled up the dismal scene with moans, and groans, and shrieks of wild despair."

Miller wasn't always such a fun fellow. He was born on February 15, 1782, in Pittsfield. When he was a young boy, his family moved to Low Hampton, New York. He only had eighteen months of schooling as a child, but he was a voracious reader. He married Lucy Smith and moved to nearby Poultney, Vermont, in 1803, where he was a farmer, a sheriff, a justice of the peace, and a respected community leader. Along with some of his neighbors in Poultney, he became skeptical of Christianity after reading the works of Thomas Paine, David Hume, and Voltaire. He dropped out of the Baptist Church and became a deist—one who believes that God created the earth but has little interest in what happens here.

Miller's view changed when he served as an infantry captain during the War of 1812.

"A fatal blow to Miller's deistic outlook was delivered at the battle of Plattsburgh, where he and only about 5,000 other Americans squared off against a reported 15,000 British troops," Richard Abanes wrote in his 1998 book, *End-Time Visions*. "Miller believed that they would experience a devastating defeat unless God intervened. After several grueling skirmishes on both land and sea, the American forces scored a decisive victory over the British fleet on September 11, 1814. It was a battle in which Miller had played a 'courageous part.' Plattsburgh ultimately spelled disaster not only for the king's invading units, but also for Miller's flagging deism. God, it seemed to Miller, had actually stepped into time and space to perform a miracle."

After the war, Miller moved his family back to a two hundred acre farm in Low Hampton. He was plagued by the bloody, apocalyptical horrors he witnessed at Plattsburgh and began to question his own beliefs about life and death, good and evil. "I was truly wretched," he later wrote, "but did not understand the cause . . . . I mourned, but without hope."

Miller, often described as a "kind and good man" who helped slaves escape to Canada on the Underground Railroad, rejoined his uncle's Baptist church and started studying the Bible. In 1816—known as the Year of No Summer because there was a frost in New England every month—Miller began an intense examination of scripture. Two years later, cherry picking from the Old Testament and using a complicated mathematical formula, he concluded "in about twenty-five years from that time all the affairs of our present state would be wound up."

Miller specifically relied on Daniel 8:14, "And he said unto me, unto two thousand and three hundred days; then shall the sanctuary be cleansed." He interpreted days to mean years. He became absolutely convinced the world would end in 1843. (Miller later clarified, in a newspaper story on January 1, 1843, that by predicting 1843, he meant the year "according to Jewish mode of computation," running from one vernal equinox to another. "I am fully convinced that sometime between March 21st, 1843, and March 21st, 1844 . . . Christ will come and bring all his saints with him.")

For a decade, Miller shared his conclusion only with close friends, but in 1831 he decided—after hearing a voice that said "Go, and tell it to the world"—that it was his duty to warn others. The following year he published his ideas serially in the *Vermont Telegraph*. In 1833, he published a widely circulated pamphlet and hit the lecture circuit to spread his vision, warning congregations throughout the Northeast of "everlasting woe" if people did not repent and prepare for the imminent return of Christ.

"You, O impenitent men and women, where will you be then?" Miller would ask in his sermons. "When heaven shall resound with the mighty song, and distant realms shall echo back the sound, where, tell me where, will you be then? In hell! O think! In hell! . . . lifting up your eyes, being in torment. Stop sinner, think! In hell. Where the beast and the false prophet are, and shall be tormented day and night, forever and ever."

In his memoirs, Miller estimated that in the next dozen years he gave more than 4,500 lectures attended by at least 500,000 people.

"Miller's sermon on prophecy was received with great enthusiasm and resulted in a deluge of invitations from other churches in New York and the northeastern United States," Abanes wrote. "Within a year, he could accept no more than half of the speaking engagement requests he received from Baptist, Methodist, and Congregational churches. . . . On more than one occasion spiritual revivals broke out in churches and towns following his dramatic presentation of apocalyptic truths."

Natural and cultural events and a general fascination with millennial speculation, reforms, revivals, and spiritualism in the early nineteenth century also contributed to Millerism's rise. In the 1830s, a cholera epidemic, a sensational meteor shower, and the blotting out of the sun in New England one day—known later to have been caused by huge forest fires in the untamed West—were seen as signs by many that the end of the world was surely near. The economic growth of the 1820s and 1830s also came to an abrupt end, with the Panic of 1837 ushering in a depression. Meanwhile, more and more Catholics, whom many Protestants reviled as a menace (Millerites even considered the Pope the anti-Christ), were coming to America through the ports of Boston and New York.

The time was ripe for doomsday predictions. But while others cried, "the end is coming," Miller actually set a date—the year between March 21, 1843, and March 21, 1844.

In 1839, Himes, a thirty-four-year-old Boston minister and abolitionist and a born promoter, teamed up with Miller to get the word out and Millerism really took off. They began publishing Miller's calculations and lectures in their Boston-based newspaper, *Signs of the Times* (later called the *Advent Herald*), and in their New York City–based the *Midnight Cry*. The great thinkers of the day, William Lloyd Garrison, Bronson Alcott, Theodore Parker, James Russell Lowell, and Ralph Waldo Emerson, all attended Millerite meetings at Himes' Chardon Street Church, although none of those reformers ended up joining. Many other people did, though. The Millerites built their own tabernacle in Boston. In 1842, Millerite camp meetings flourished, some under a tent that held more than four thousand people and was said to be the largest ever constructed. The Millerites attracted crowds with three-foot-by-six-foot charts depicting colorful, bizarre images of the Apocalypse—angels blowing trumpets, lions with wings, dragons with seven heads, grotesque beasts with bared teeth.

"In the age of P. T Barnum, Americans seemed to have a boundless appetite for spectacle and entertainment, and the tent turned out to be an inspired advertising ploy," Catherine A. Brekus wrote in her 1998 book *Strangers & Pilgrims: Female Preaching in America, 1740–1845*. "Barnum himself, the master of humbug, later imitated the Millerites by buying an enormous tent for his 'Greatest Show on Earth.' Whether or not Barnum ever attended a Millerite meeting, he knew expert salesmanship when he saw it. Many of his circus posters, with their pictures of ferocious-looking beasts, looked remarkably like the Millerites' prophetic charts."

In 1843, Millerism reached a fever pitch. The number of Millerites, or Adventists as they were also called, has been estimated at 50,000; some put the number at 100,000 or more. Pockets of Millerism sprang up in Canada and Great Britain. Publisher Horace Greeley in New York and other journalists in Boston and Philadelphia warned that Miller's doomsday

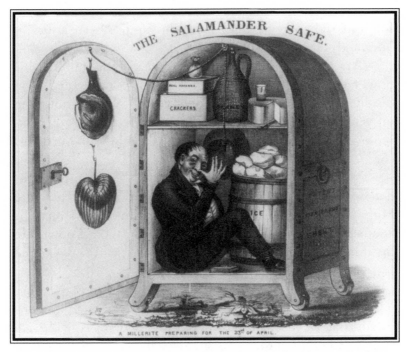

A cartoon mocking the Millerites, published in 1843 by Thomas Sinclair
in Philadelphia

prediction constituted a huge public threat. "If your preaching
drives people into despair or insanity, you are responsible for
the consequences," lexicographer Noah Webster wrote to the
preacher.

As the March end date grew near, some men stopped
working, some farmers stopped farming, businesses closed,
and Millerites gave all of their money and possessions to heirs
and even strangers.

"On March 21, 1844, some of the more fanatical Millerites
completely lost control," Abanes wrote. "A Boston journalist
who had been following the story reported to the *New York
Herald* that many Millerites had actually jumped from roofs
and treetops in hopes of timing their leaps with Christ's return.

But Jesus did not return and those who jumped 'were critically hurt, and some fell to their deaths.'"

After March 21 came—and went—the public and press had a field day and the Millerites were ridiculed. The headline of one Boston newspaper read: "What!—not gone up yet?—We thought you'd gone up! Aren't you going up soon?—Wife didn't go up and leave you behind to burn, did she?"

Miller, who was in poor health, was embarrassed and determined to figure out how he had miscalculated. He wrote Himes a letter about children ridiculing him on the streets. In another letter he wrote, "I confess my error, and acknowledge my disappointment [however] I still believe that the day of the Lord is near, even at the door."

Some of Miller's followers gave up, but most did not. Though desperate and hurt, they found solace in Miller's words that "soon our time, and all prophetic days, will have been filled." Numerous Christian, Methodist, and Free Will Baptist congregations divided over Miller's prediction. Excommunications, "disfellowships," and schisms occurred and some Adventists established churches of their own.

In August, Millerite Samuel S. Snow's recalculation, called the "Seventh Month Message" (a reference to the seventh month in the Jewish calendar), set the end date as October 22. It took hold at a camp meeting in New Hampshire and quickly spread like wind-whipped hellfire through the Adventist churches and beyond. Luther Boutelle, the Millerite lecturer from Groton, recalled, "Such a oneness of faith was never before witnessed; certainly not in modern times. All that did speak spoke the same things. Solemn, yet joyful. Jesus coming! We to meet him!"

Neither Miller nor Himes endorsed the new date at first. But tens of thousands of Adventists, after so much doubt and embarrassment, seized on it "with great enthusiasm," according to Paul Conklin in his 1997 book, *American Originals: Homemade Varieties of Christianity*.

"The date quickly became a self-fulfilling prophecy," Conklin wrote. "Its impact was so great and the fervor of the new revival so irresistible that Himes and Miller finally capitulated in early October, under conviction that the Holy Spirit had to be behind such wonderful effects."

On October 6, Miller wrote in the *Advent Herald*. "I see a glory in the seventh month which I never saw before. . . . I see a beauty, a harmony, and an agreement in the scriptures. . . . I am almost home, Glory! Glory!! Glory!! . . . . If he does not come within 20 or 25 days, I shall feel twice the disappointment I did this spring."

On October 12, Himes published what he expected to be the last edition of the *Advent Herald*. "We therefore find our work is now finished and that all we have to do is to go out to meet the Bridegroom and to trim our lamps accordingly. . . . Your blood be upon your own heads."

On October 22, the faithful made ready. Millerites in Salem marched in white robes to Gallows Hill where Puritans had hanged witches 152 years earlier. Thousands gathered at the Millerite tabernacle in Boston. Some believers in central Massachusetts scaled Mount Wachusett, while others climbed trees or simply waited in their homes.

"The eventful day at last arrived," Henry Clair of New Bedford, who was a child in 1844, told historian Sears in 1921. "The forenoon passed away and the dinner hour arrived, but none of the elder ones ate much food. . . . About nine o'clock my mother's father put on his ascension robe and sat at the window so as to be all ready to ascend up. Everything was quiet, and nothing could be heard but the beating of our hearts. . . . Then some of the elder ones ventured to the door, opened it very cautiously and peeked out, and as they saw nothing unusual going on, they took fresh courage and went out, and walked around the house and went in again, and held a consultation about the affair, and came to the conclusion that William Miller had made a slight mistake in the time. My mother's father sat near the window with his ascension robe on until three o'clock in the morning, then got up and went about his daily affairs."

Few took the Great Disappointment so well.

"Still in the cold world," Luther Boutelle wrote in his memoirs. "No deliverance—the Lord had not come. . . . It was a humiliating thing, and we all felt it alike."

Joseph Bates, a friend of Miller's, wrote: "I had been a respected citizen, and had with much confidence exhorted the people to be ready for the expected change. . . . If the earth could have opened and swallowed me up, it would have been sweetness compared to the distress I felt."

Millerism was dead, buried in a sea of ridicule. Some adherents returned to their old churches. Many joined the Shakers, another New England–based doomsday sect that gained new members only through recruitment since they practiced celibacy. At least a dozen branches of Adventism grew out of Millerism, some almost overnight after the Great Disappointment, and many survive to this day. Ellen G. White, prophet and spiritual leader of the Seventh-day Adventist Church, which today claims 8.5 million members worldwide, later compared Miller to John the Baptist in her writing.

After October 22, 1844, Miller quit his active ministry although he remained involved in Adventism. He still insisted the time was close at hand and he was cast out of the Baptist church in Low Hampton. Within three years he was blind. In May 1849, he was too sick to attend the Advent Conference in New York City. Instead, he sent a letter that said, "My belief is unshaken in the correctness of the conclusions I have arrived at. . . . We may not know the precise time, but I entreat of you all to be prepared for the approaching crisis."

He died seven months later, three days after Himes made a final visit. Miller, unable to speak for more than a few moments, proclaimed "Elder Himes has come—I love Elder Himes." He told another deathbed visitor, "Tell them we are right. The coming of the Lord draweth nigh; but they must be patient, and wait for him."

"The closing scene finally came," eyewitness Sylvester Bliss wrote in his 1853 *Memoirs of William Miller.* "On the 20th of December, in the morning, it was manifest to all that he must soon depart. During the morning he made no particular conversation, but would break forth in expressions like the following: 'Mighty to save!' 'Oh, I long to be there!' 'Victory! Victory!' 'Shouting in death!'"

Miller left behind his wife and eight children. His home is now a historical site maintained by the Seventh-day Adventist church.

Himes died in South Dakota in 1895, escaping "at last from the gibes and ridicule incurred by the failure of the prophecy" according to Clara Endicott Sears. Fifteen years earlier, "he suddenly renounced the doctrine which he had been so instrumental in spreading and took orders as a clergyman of the Episcopal Church." Even though he became an Episcopalian in his later years, Himes carried at least one of the Millerites' 1844 beliefs to the grave—he asked his bishop to bury him in an elevated spot in Mount Pleasant Cemetery in Sioux Falls, according to Sears, "because he wanted to be on the top of a hill when Gabriel blows his trumpet."

9

Joseph Palmer, 1789–1873
Persecuted for Wearing the Beard

One of the most bizarre incidents of prejudice to rear its head—or, more accurately, show its face—occurred in central Massachusetts in 1830.

The story of Joseph Palmer's persecution is well documented. And just in case we ever forget, there's a raised replica of Palmer's face and free-flowing beard carved into his white marble tombstone in the Evergreen Cemetery in Leominster. It's visible from Route 13—just look over the wall seventy-five yards north of the intersection with Route 12. You'll have to get out of your car and walk closer to read the inscription: "Persecuted for wearing the beard."

It's hard for us to imagine the furor Joe Palmer's beard caused in 1830, but in the early nineteenth century in America, few men, except those in the young country's tiny Jewish community, wore beards. Although the Pilgrims and Puritans and other early explorers and colonists were almost all bearded, hair had pretty much disappeared from the face of America by 1720, and American men stayed clean shaven for more than one hundred years after that. Not one signer of the Declaration of Independence wore a beard or mustache. The beard would reappear before the Civil War—Lincoln, Lee, and Grant all sported full facial hair—but during Joe Palmer's younger days virtually no one wore a beard.

And therein lies the story.

Joe Palmer was born in 1789 and grew up as one of fourteen children on a family farm in NoTown, the unincorporated land between Leominster and Fitchburg where Leominster's NoTown Reservoir is visible from Route 2 today. Palmer's father fought in the American Revolution and Palmer himself fought against the British in the War of 1812. After the war, he returned to his family farm in NoTown, where he was known as "an honest, kindly man and good citizen, deeply religious but tolerant, a man of many intellectual interests," according to a 1945 story in *The American Scholar*.

Palmer was always a nonconformist though, a reformer and strong willed. He was an early abolitionist. He angered many in Fitchburg in 1818 by posting his wedding banns to the widow Nancy Tenney on a pine tree. He reasoned, NoTown had no meeting house and thus no government. He further angered his Fitchburg neighbors as an early temperance advocate by refusing to serve rum to his hired hands. And before he turned forty, Palmer's religious beliefs led to his most momentous decision.

"He admired the Biblical patriarchs like Moses, and Moses had a flowing beard," Irving Wallace wrote in *Ramparts* in 1973. "He admired the Messiah, and Jesus Christ had an impressive beard. So Joseph Palmer decided to grow a beard. And in this facially hairless land of the free, Palmer's flowing Biblical beard was one of a kind, the only one known from Atlantic to Pacific."

Actually, there was one other beard-wearer right in central Massachusetts, according to Palmer's son Thomas, who was interviewed by the *Boston Daily Globe* in 1884.

"Father . . . wore at that time a long beard, and he and Silas Lamson, an old scythe-snath maker of Sterling, were the only men known in this section of the country as wearing beards," Thomas Palmer told the reporter.

Lamson, whose family had prospered in Sterling by manufacturing a curved-handle scythe that he invented, was a story himself. His sons formed a successful cutlery company in Shelburne Falls in the western part of the state, but Silas became a "wanderer" and for a time lived on the streets of Boston. He became well known as an eccentric who would dress head to toe in white and rail loudly at abolitionists' meetings. He was often called "Father Time Lamson" or "the White Quaker." His *New York Times* obituary in 1855 began, "A correspondent for the *Boston Herald* announces the death of Silas Lamson, so well known as a monomaniac."

Joe Palmer's beard also earned him nicknames—and ire.

"Everybody shaved clean in those days, and to wear whiskers in any form was worse than a disgrace, it was a sin," his son recalled. "Father was hooted at on the street, talked about at the grocery, intimidated by his fellow men and labored with by the clergy to shave, but to no purpose. The stronger the opposition, the firmer his determination. He was accosted once by Rev. George Trask, the antitobacconist, who said indignantly: 'Palmer, why don't you shave and not go round looking like the devil?' He replied: 'Mr. Trask, are you not mistaken in your comparison of personages? I have never seen a picture of the ruler of the sulphurous regions with much of a beard, but if I remember correctly, Jesus wore a beard not unlike mine.'"

It wouldn't be the last time Joe Palmer would have a run-in with Trask.

Whenever Joe and his beard ventured off the farm into Fitchburg, teenage boys threw rocks and screamed catcalls at him. Vandals broke windows in the Palmers' house. Because of the beard, Joe Palmer became known as "Old Jew Palmer" even though he was a Baptist.

"The older inhabitants of Harvard, Sterling, Leominster, Fitchburg, and other neighboring towns can remember 'Old Jew Palmer,' who 50 years ago was persecuted, despised, jeered at, regarded almost as a fiend incarnate; who was known far and wide as a human monster, and with whose name mothers used to frighten their children when they were unruly," the *Globe* reporter wrote in 1884. "'Old Jew Palmer,' as he was universally called, was the most abused and persecuted man these parts ever knew, and all because he insisted upon wearing a beard."

The defining moment came when Joe Palmer went to church in Fitchburg in 1830 and Reverend Trask refused to give him the communion bread and wine.

"Cut to the quick at such injustice, and with the blood surging to his face, he arose and strode up to the Communion table where the Sacraments were, and lifting the cup to his lips drank from it," Clara Endicott Sears wrote in her book *Bronson Alcott's Fruitlands*. "And, turning to the shocked and abashed clergyman and his congregation, shouted in a loud voice and with flashing eyes: 'I love my Jesus as well, and better, than any of you do!'"

The incident quickly made Palmer one of the most reviled men in New England and the harassment increased. Four men jumped him while he was delivering cucumbers and meat to the Fitchburg Hotel a short time later. They threw him down on the hotel's stone steps and tried to shave him. Despite injuring his back, the forty-year-old Palmer fought savagely. He managed to reach for a pocketknife, and, swinging it wildly, cut two of his assailants on their legs. Neither was injured seriously, but the attackers fled, leaving Palmer's magnificent beard intact.

The two men then swore out complaints against Palmer for his "unprovoked attack." A judge found him guilty, but Palmer refused, on principle, to pay a small fine. He was incarcerated in the Worcester City Jail where he spent more than a year. Twice, he fought off jailers and other prisoners who tried to shave him.

"In jail, Joe wrote letters in which he stated that he was in there not for assault but because he chose to wear whiskers— which was unquestionably the case," Stewart Holbrook wrote in *The American Scholar* piece.

Thomas Palmer gave his dad's passionate letters to the *Worcester Spy* for publication. Other newspapers throughout the Northeast, including the *Boston Daily Globe,* picked them up.

"Suddenly," Wallace wrote, "Palmer's arguments about individual freedom and human rights began to give many citizens second thoughts . . . Sympathy began to build."

The Worcester sheriff realized he had a martyr on his hands and ordered Palmer released, although he still had not paid his fine. Palmer refused to leave, however, until he was fully absolved, and also because he thought the jailers had cheated him out of money he had paid for food and coal to heat his cell. His wife and Thomas had rented an apartment near the jail and were eager to go back to Fitchburg, but to Joe Palmer, principles were everything.

"He far out-stayed his sentence," the *Boston Daily Globe* reporter wrote. "The sheriff and jailers, tired of having him there, begged him to leave. Even his mother, Margaret Palmer, wrote to him, 'not to be so set.' But nothing could move him. He said they had put him in there, and they would have to take him out, as he would not walk out. They finally carried him out in his chair and placed it on the sidewalk."

Now Palmer had the respect of the nation's reformers and radicals and, undaunted by continued harassment in Fitchburg, he turned his attention to the abolition movement. He met with William Lloyd Garrison and Wendell Phillips and other key reformers who reportedly found him a bit odd but full of common sense. He began to attend abolition and temperance events in Boston and can be spotted—perhaps with Silas Lamson because the reference is plural—in Ralph Waldo Emerson's description of the Chardon Street Convention in 1840.

"If the assembly was disorderly, it was picturesque," Emerson wrote. "Madmen, madwomen, men with beards, Dunkers, Muggletonians, Comeouters, Groaners, Agrarians, Seventh-Day Baptists, Quakers, Abolitionists, Calvinists, Unitarians and Philosophers—all came successively to the top, and seized their moment, if not their hour, wherein to chide, or pray, or preach or protest."

In 1901, Thomas Palmer, then eighty-one, told the *Leom-inster Enterprise* that he recalled going to Boston as a young man to attend one of the abolition meetings and the police being called to clear Tremont Street because so many people had gathered to look at his dad's free-flowing beard.

"It was so unusual to see a man wearing one, and especially such a one as he sported," Thomas Palmer said. "Why, he was looked upon as a monstrosity. When asked once why he wore it, he said he would tell if anyone could tell him why some men would, from 52 to 365 times a year, scrape their face from their nose to their neck."

Joe Palmer joined Bronson Alcott's Transcendentalist commune at Fruitlands in Harvard in 1843. He donated much of the commune's furniture from his farm, fifteen miles to the west, and offered to run the Con-Sociate Family's one hundred acre farm without pay. That was a good thing, too, because Alcott and Charles Lane, who founded the utopian community, were great abstract thinkers but had no idea how to actually feed themselves. Transcendentalism, a movement of New England writers and thinkers that emerged in the 1830s and is based on the work of eighteenth-century German philosopher Immanuel Kant, holds that people are born good, and through intuition and observing nature, they can become closer to God. Hard work, at least in Alcott's and Lane's case, was not a factor.

"Here we prosecute our efforts to initiate a Family in harmony with the primitive instincts of man," Lane and Alcott wrote in a joint letter to *The Dial*, a Transcendentalist magazine, on June 10, 1843.

Alcott, born in 1799 on a flax farm in Connecticut, had never actually farmed. He had taught himself to read and was a lifelong educator. As a teacher, he included art, music, physical education and nature studies in his classes at a time when no one else did. His progressive methods and anti–organized religion stance were often considered too radical and he lost many teaching positions—the Alcott family moved more than twenty times in thirty years.

In the spring of 1843, Alcott and his wife Abby and their four children formed the Fruitlands commune with Lane, and the financial backing of Emerson. They named it Fruitlands because they intended to live off the fruits of the land. Nine other adults, including Palmer, soon arrived.

Fruitlands was one of many experiments in utopian communal living attempted in the nineteenth century. The best known one attempted by writers and philosophers in Massachusetts was the two hundred acre Brook Farm in West Roxbury, where George Ripley, a former Unitarian minister and later a literary critic for the *New York Tribune*, attempted to put the plain living theories of Emerson into practice from 1841 to 1847. Brook Farm had about one hundred members, including intellectuals, carpenters, farmers, shoemakers, and printers. Everyone worked up to ten hours each day, whether in farming or other industries. A fire in 1846, followed by a lawsuit filed by writer Nathaniel Hawthorne to reclaim his investment, spelled the end for Brook Farm.

Bronson Alcott and Lane visited Brook Farm, as well as a Shaker community already established in the hills of Harvard, before they embarked on the Fruitlands experiment.

"Why, then, did [Alcott] not go with Ripley?" asked Lindsay Swift in the 1900 book, *Brook Farm: Its Members, Scholars, and Visitors*. "There is no sure answer, but we may, in fairness, suppose that he would have stayed long away from a project which involved 300 days' labor in each year, with an average of 54 working hours to each week of six days. This philosopher would gladly have conversed under a noonday sun until the sweat poured down his face, but for physical toil he had no affinity. The nebular state of most projects was definite enough for Mr. Alcott."

That turned out to be a real problem at Fruitlands.

The Alcotts and Lane believed all contact with social institutions corrupted man's innate goodness. They considered commerce and the desire for material goods to be demeaning. They saw industrial work as particularly bad for the soul.

The Con-Sociates became the strictest of vegetarians—they wouldn't even use honey because it belonged to the bees or milk because it belonged to cows. Their plan for Fruitlands was that the members would work in the fields by day and discuss philosophy at night.

They had the discussion part down, but not the work part. Joe Palmer was the only one with any farming experience. The other adult Con-Sociates included a baker who would eventually become a Catholic priest, a nudist, a man who swore at everyone to assert his freedom, and Abram Wood, a cooper who had previously been in an insane asylum and who insisted on being called Wood Abram. The only adult woman in the group besides Abby Alcott, Ann Page, was expelled for eating a piece of fish.

Ardent abolitionists, Bronson Alcott and Lane didn't even think it right to use oxen or mules to pull plows. But, being intellectuals not given to hard physical work, they had no intention of doing it themselves. Palmer is credited with keeping the experiment going for as long as it lasted—for starters he went home shortly after his arrival and returned with a team of oxen.

"He was, in fact, the only sensible male in that wondrous experiment," Holbrook wrote. Palmer appears in Louisa May Alcott's *Transcendental Wild Oats* as Moses White. Louisa May, Bronson's daughter who was ten at the time of the Fruitlands experiment, is of course, most famous for her book *Little Women*.

The Fruitlands experiment started to fall apart as the Con-Sociates began bickering. When a visitor asked Abby Alcott if the commune had any beasts of burden she replied sarcastically, "Only one woman." When Bronson Alcott and Lane left in the fall to unsuccessfully try to recruit new members, Joe Palmer and Abby Alcott were the only ones left to bring in the meager harvest.

The Fruitlands experiment lasted just seven months. Without sufficient food, supplies, or firewood, the Alcotts—with deeply depressed Bronson the last to leave—returned to Concord in January 1844.

Joe Palmer soon bought the farm and moved there with Nancy. For more than twenty years, the Palmers welcomed all visitors—including hobos, famous writers, and reformers—to their own version of utopia at Fruitlands. Emerson came to visit Palmer often in Harvard. The Palmers always had a pot of beans on the stove and plenty of bread to offer. All were welcome to stay, so long as they didn't drink alcohol. His neighbors derisively called it "Old Palmer's Home for Tramps."

Thomas Palmer became a dentist in Fitchburg and, like his father, never shaved his beard. In interviews seventeen years apart, he told the *Boston Daily Globe* and *Leominster Enterprise* that as a boy he had been embarrassed to be the son of "Old Jew Palmer" but as the years went by he came to admire his dad's integrity, spirit, and courage. Thomas Palmer was the one who commissioned the six-foot tall obelisk in Evergreen Cemetery under which his parents are buried.

"The doctor looks back upon those days proudly, as he realizes that his sire was right and that the world has endorsed the ways and ideas of the old man, instead of the old man bowing to the absurd whim of the world," the *Globe* reported in 1884.

Joe Palmer died in 1873. By then, the great Civil War had been fought, the slaves had been freed, and virtually every man in the United States wore a beard. In fact, young women in that era often repeated the saying, "Kissing a man without whiskers is like eating an egg without salt."

One day in his old age, Palmer was walking down the street in Fitchburg when he spotted Reverend Trask. Even the minister who had refused Palmer communion some four decades earlier wore a beard by then. Witnesses reported Palmer approached the clergyman, stroked his own beard and said, "Knowest thou that thy redeemer liveth?"

In 1914, author, historian, and preservationist Clara Endicott Sears restored the Fruitlands farmhouse and opened it as

Joe Palmer's grave in Leominster, Massachussetts

a museum. In 1915, she compiled her book, *Bronson Alcott's Fruitlands*, which includes Louisa May Alcott's *Transcendental Wild Oats*. Fruitlands, in a beautiful hillside setting overlooking the Nashoba Valley of central Massachusetts, contains portraits of Joe and Nancy Palmer, manuscripts and artifacts of many Transcendentalist writers, and also houses Shaker and Native American historical museums and a New England art museum.

10

David Walker, circa 1796–1830
"Are we Men?"

Who—or what—killed David Walker?

On August 6, 1830, his lifeless body was discovered in the doorway of his used clothing store on Brattle Street in Boston. Walker's death certificate said he died of "consumption," the same tuberculosis that killed his twenty-one-month-old daughter Lydia just a week earlier, and had recently claimed the lives of numerous Bostonians.

Many of his fellow blacks, however, believed that Walker had been poisoned. After all, slave owners in Georgia not long before had put a price on his head, and many whites in the South feared Walker's incendiary pen so desperately that three states—Georgia, Louisiana, and North Carolina—had hastily passed legislation making it a crime to teach blacks—free or enslaved—to read or write.

Almost two centuries later, the mystery of how David Walker died remains—no autopsy was ever performed. What is not a mystery is the effect of the seventy-six-page pamphlet that Walker first self-published in 1829. The righteous, inflammatory language of *David Walker's Appeal in Four Articles; Together with a Preamble, to the Coloured Citizens of the World, but in Particular, and Very Expressly, to Those of the United States of America* threw the South into a panic. In his *Appeal*, Walker denounced any Americans and Christians—especially Thomas

Jefferson—who hypocritically preached liberty while condoning slavery. He also denounced Henry Clay and others in the American Colonization Society who wanted to send blacks back to Africa. Walker called on slaves to rebel, to rise up and reclaim their dignity and their rightful place in the America they had built with their "blood and tears," or to at least die trying.

"Now, I ask you, had not you rather be killed than to be a slave to a tyrant, who takes the life of your mother, wife, and dear little children?" he wrote. "Look upon your mother, wife and children, and answer God Almighty! and believe this, that it is no more harm for you to kill a man, who is trying to kill you, than it is for you to take a drink of water when thirsty. . . . Are we MEN! !—I ask you, O my brethren, are we MEN? Did our Creator make us to be slaves to dust and ashes like ourselves?"

In the 1820s, Boston Harbor was a bustling seaport. Black and white sailors frequented Walker's clothing store near the waterfront.

"Walker used this fact to distribute his antislavery literature to the South and all over the world," wrote Darryl Scriven in his 2007 book, *A Dealer of Old Clothes*. "He would 'plant' this material in the jacket and trouser pockets of suspecting and unsuspecting wayfarers to reach those who were in solidarity and/or moral agreement with the abolitionist cause. Whatever destinations the sailors had, the pamphlet accompanied them along the way. . . . Those on their way home in the South formed an information network that spread Walker's abolitionist sentiments."

In less than a year, the *Appeal* had gone through three printings. Across the South, state legislatures met to talk about ways to prevent its distribution. "The Legislature in two states have been frightened by a few dozen pamphlets written by a Negro who deals in old clothes," a *Nikes' Register* editorialist wrote on February 27, 1830. After authorities in Savannah found one sailor with sixty copies of the *Appeal*, the state of

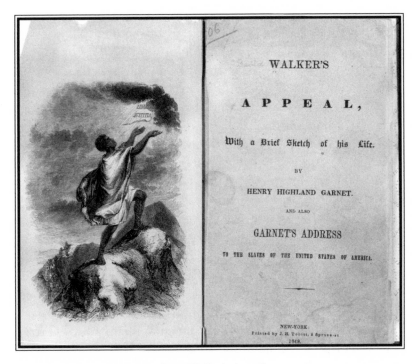

Frontispiece and title page from *Walker's Appeal*

Georgia forbade black sailors from coming ashore while their ships were in harbor, and several Southern states passed laws charging anyone found with multiple copies of distributing seditious literature.

"This little book produced more commotion among slaveholders than any volume of its size that was ever issued from an American press," wrote Henry Highland Garnet, a fellow black abolitionist and Walker's first biographer. "They saw that it was a bold attack upon their idolatry, and that too by a black man who once lived among them. It was merely a smooth stone which this David took up, yet it terrified a host of Goliaths. When the fame of this book reached the South, the poor, cowardly, pusillanimous tyrants, grew pale behind their cotton bags, and armed themselves to the teeth. They set watches to look after their happy and contented slaves. The Governor of Georgia wrote to the Hon. Harrison Grey Otis, the Mayor of Boston, requesting him to suppress the Appeal. His Honor replied to the Southern Censor that he had no power nor disposition to hinder Mr. Walker from pursuing a lawful course in the utterance of his thoughts. A company of Georgia men then bound themselves by an oath, that they would eat as little as possible until they had killed the youthful author. They also offered a reward of a thousand dollars for his head, and ten times as much for the live Walker."

Eric Foner, a Columbia University history professor, said in an interview with Public Broadcasting that Walker began the movement that would culminate with Lincoln's Emancipation Proclamation during the Civil War.

"Historians traditionally date the beginning of the modern Abolitionist Movement—the movement for the immediate abolition of slavery—from 1831, when William Lloyd Garrison began publication of the *Liberator*, the great abolitionist newspaper in Boston," Foner said. "But I think there's a good argument to be made that, really, 1829 should be the beginning of this movement. And that was with the publication of *David Walker's Appeal*."

The Father of the Abolition Movement is a lofty title, especially for a man about whom so much is still unclear. Not only is his cause of death a mystery, but much about Walker's early life is also unknown. Garnet interviewed Walker's widow for his 1848 biography, but even she did not know that much about her husband's childhood, other than that he had been born in Wilmington, North Carolina, and that he was the son of a free black woman and a slave, and that his father died before he was born. A probable typographical mistake in Garnet's profile put Walker's date of birth at 1785, but later historians believe he was more probably born in 1796. Three newspapers, the *Boston Daily Courier*, the *Boston Daily Advertiser*, and the *New England Palladium*, all listed his age as thirty-three in 1830 when he died.

By North Carolina law, a child assumed his mother's status, so Walker was born free, although being a free black in North Carolina at the turn of the nineteenth century was not much better than being a slave. Revolts had already occurred on slave ships and in 1785 in Haiti. In 1800, a rebellion by one thousand slaves in Virginia armed only with clubs was rapidly suppressed. Their leader, a man simply called Gabriel, and fifteen other blacks were executed. By the 1820s, some Southern slave apologists still insisted they slept without fear, but others told a different truth.

"There was no escape from the realities represented by the radical black presence in America," historian Kenneth Greenberg wrote. "Thus private and public writings from the South continually referred to deep levels of fear—fear of insurrection, fear of death at black hands, fear of black life, fear of blackness, fear of repressed and frightening white desires. Usually it came out in references to 'an internal foe,' or 'the dangerous internal population,' or 'the enemy in our very bosom,' perhaps revealing more than the writers ever knew."

Southerners greatly feared that free blacks, especially those who had been in the North, would foment rebellion among the enslaved, and passed laws limiting free blacks' contact with their "happy" slaves. A law in North Carolina required all free blacks to wear a badge embroidered with the word "Free" on their left shoulders. In those days, throughout the South—and even in the North—almost all white Americans saw blacks as inferior. Brutality was ubiquitous. In his *Appeal*, Walker wrote about watching a young slave boy who was forced to strip his mother naked and whip her into a bloody dead pulp, and of another slave being forced to lash his pregnant wife until she aborted her baby.

"If I remain in this bloody land, I will not live long," Walker wrote. "This is not the place for me, no, I must leave this part of the country. It will be a great trial for me to live on the same soil where so many men are in slavery, certainly I cannot remain where I must hear their chains continually, and, where I must encounter the results of their hypocritical enslavers. Go, I must."

Walker moved to Charleston, South Carolina, where many free blacks lived and worked. He joined the African Methodist Church, and may have been there in 1822 during the planning of a slave rebellion led by Denmark Vesey, a free black man. Informants tipped off the white authorities and Vesey and thirty-five other African Americans were hanged. Walker then traveled through the South and to Philadelphia, where he became acquainted with Bishop Richard Allen, a former slave, founder of the African Methodist Episcopal Church, and a leading opponent of colonization. "This land which we have watered with our tears and our blood, is now our mother country, and we are well satisfied to stay where wisdom abounds and the gospel is free," Allen wrote. Walker traveled to New York and Baltimore before moving to Boston around 1825.

Shortly after arriving in Boston, Walker—described by Garnet as dark-complexioned with loose hair and "being 6 feet in height, slender and well proportioned"— opened his clothing store. He began assisting fugitive slaves and attending abolitionist meetings—at that time almost exclusively black. He also began to intensely study and read scripture, history, and even the papers of the founding fathers, including Thomas Jefferson's *Notes on the State of Virginia* that claimed blacks "were not of the human family" but descended originally "from the tribes of Monkeys or Orang-Outangs."

Walker wooed and, in 1826, wed Eliza Butler, a native black Bostonian. They lived on the north slope of Beacon Hill, the center of the city's small but vibrant black community. (About two thousand free blacks made up 3 percent of Boston's population at the time.) Walker joined Boston's African Methodist Episcopal Church and the Prince Hall African Masonic Lodge and helped found the Massachusetts General Colored Association. In March 1827, he began writing for, and selling subscriptions to, *Freedom's Journal,* the first national newspaper published for and by blacks. He became the Boston correspondent for the New York–based paper, which was devoted to abolition and the defeat of the American Colonization Society, and he held that position for the two years the *Journal* was published.

In 1828, Eliza gave birth to a daughter, Lydia. By then, Walker had become one of the city's leading black orators and its most outspoken and eloquent black radical. In that same year, he delivered a series of four blistering lectures to the colored association. He self-published those essays in September 1829 in his *Appeal to the Colored Citizens of the World*.

"Having traveled over a considerable portion of these United States," he wrote, "and having, in the course of my travels taken the most accurate observations of things as they exist—the result of my observations has warranted the full and unshakened conviction, that we, (colored people of these United States) are the most degraded, wretched, and abject set of beings that ever lived since the world began, and I pray God, that none like us ever may live again until time shall be no more."

In his *Appeal*, Walker poured out his soul and exhorted blacks to "kill or be killed." He warned white Americans that "unless you speedily alter your course, *you* and your *Country are gone!!!!!!*"

Like pellets from a shotgun, the ink from Walker's pen slammed into numerous targets—hypocritical white ministers, murderous slave owners, even fearful blacks. "If you can only get courage into the blacks, I do declare it, that one good black man can put to death six white men," he wrote. "The reason is, the blacks, once you get them started, they glory in death."

Walker demanded white Americans to compare their own language in the Declaration of Independence "with your cruelties and murders inflicted by your cruel and unmerciful fathers and yourselves on our fathers and on us, men who have never given your fathers or you the least provocation!!!" He asked: Were the colonists' "sufferings under Great Britain one hundredth part as cruel and tyrannical" as what slaves endured?

Walker saved particular venom for the American Colonization Society. "America is more our country than it is the whites," he wrote. "We have enriched it with our *blood and tears* . . . will they drive us from our property and homes, which we have earned with our *blood?*"

Walker did not vilify all Caucasians in his *Appeal*. "He was impelled not by a hatred of white America, but by a profound love and compassion for his people," Greenberg wrote. In the *Appeal,* Walker thanked the whites "who have volunteered their services for our redemption. . . . Though we are unable to compensate them for their labours, we nevertheless thank them from the bottom of our hearts, and have our eyes steadfastly fixed upon them, and their labors of love for God and man."

Walker's unique marketing strategy—sewing copies of the pamphlet into the jackets of southbound sailors—proved remarkably effective. Within weeks, the *Appeal* was discovered in Savannah, Georgia, and copies were soon found throughout the South, from Virginia to Louisiana. The white South went into panic mode, quickly passing anti-literacy laws and banning blacks—including free blacks—from having contact with incoming sailors. Many abolitionists, even some blacks, thought Walker had gone too far. All previous abolition tracts, noted Robin Kadison Berson in 1994's *Marching to a Different Drummer: Unrecognized Heroes of American History,* had taken a more supplicant stance.

"*Walker's Appeal* represented a radical departure from these antecedents," Berson wrote. "For the first time, an African American addressed other African Americans, not whites. He did not apologize, petition meekly, or humbly assure his 'betters' that he had no desire for economic and social equality."

At a Boston dinner party celebrating the *Appeal's* first edition, Eliza and friends concerned about his safety implored Walker to flee to Canada.

"I will stand my ground—somebody must die in this cause," Walker responded. "I may be doomed to the stake and the fire, or to the scaffold tree, but it is not in me to falter if I can promote the work of emancipation."

In less than a year, he would be dead. Before he died, he published a second and third edition, each more militant than the previous. On July 30, 1830, in the midst of a tuberculosis epidemic in Boston, his infant daughter Lydia died. On August 6, Walker was discovered dead in the doorway of his store. Eliza was pregnant at the time—David Walker's son Edward would become one of the first black lawyers in the Bay State and, in 1866, the first black man elected to the Massachusetts Legislature.

Even after Walker's death, reprinting and distribution of the *Appeal* continued throughout the South, where blacks accounted for 40 percent of the population. North Carolina governor John Owen criticized Walker's pamphlet as "an open appeal to [the black's] natural love of liberty . . . and . . . totally subversive of all subordination in our slaves." Rumors of slave insurrection plots spread among petrified white residents in Walker's home state.

"Many communities petitioned . . . Owen for protection as their slaves became 'almost uncontrollable,'" according to the *Dictionary of North Carolina Biography*. "The governor sent a copy of the *Appeal* to the legislature when it met in November 1830 and urged that it consider measures to avert the dangerous consequences that were predicted. Meeting in secret session, the legislature enacted the most repressive measures ever passed in North Carolina to control slaves and free blacks."

On January 8, 1831, in one of his first editions of the *Liberator*, white abolitionist leader and Boston publisher William Lloyd Garrison decried Walker's call for violence, but acknowledged its source.

"Believing, as we do, that men should never do evil that good may come . . . we deprecate the spirit and tendency of this *Appeal*," Garrison wrote. "Nevertheless, it is not for the American people, as a nation, to denounce it as bloody or monstrous. Mr. Walker but pays them in their own coin . . . if any people were ever justified in throwing off the yoke of their tyrants, the slaves are that people. It is not we, but our guilty country-men, who put arguments into the mouths, and swords into the hands of the slaves."

One year after Walker's death, his call to arms bore deadly fruit. Nat Turner, a slave and "prophet," led a bloody slave revolt in Virginia. Quaker abolitionist Benjamin Lundy wrote that it was "probable" *Walker's Appeal* had goaded Turner into action. Certainly, *Walker's Appeal* established the climate.

"As a result of it, much 'unrest and plotting' were noted in the black community," Greenberg wrote. "Early in 1830, a report from Wilmington announced that 'there has been much shooting of negroes in Wilmington recently, in consequence of symptoms of liberty having been discovered among them.' . . . And what of Nat Turner? Did Walker's *Appeal* ever reach him as he waited for the proper sign in Southampton County? No record exists of that contact, if it ever occurred. But the contact was not necessary, for Nat Turner had long been convinced that the God of Walker's *Appeal* had always been in Southampton."

After a solar eclipse and another day on which the sun appeared bluish-green, Turner made his move. On August 21 and 22, Turner and about forty other slaves went from house to house on horseback, stabbing, clubbing, and shooting to death almost sixty whites, mostly women and children. The state of Virginia subsequently executed fifty-five blacks convicted of involvement, and white mobs murdered almost two hundred more, many who had nothing to do with Turner. In the pan-icked flames created by Walker's *Appeal* and then fanned by Turner's Rebellion, slaves as far away as North Carolina were falsely accused of having complicity in the insurrection and executed.

Nat Turner eluded capture until the end of October. He was tried in Southampton County on November 5. Six days later, he was hanged—and then skinned.

In his confession, Turner said God ordered him to bring judgment against whites through a vision in which "white spirits and black spirits engaged in battle, and the sun was darkened—the thunder rolled in the heavens, and blood flowed in streams." In a letter to South Carolina governor James Hamilton, Virginia governor John Floyd blamed Nat Turner's Revolt on the "Yankee population" in general and Yankee peddlers and traders in particular who shared Christianity with the slaves and taught them that all are born free and equal, and "that white people rebelled against England to obtain freedom, so have blacks a right to do."

In 1859, John Brown, a white, deeply religious New England abolitionist, studied the tactics of Nat Turner and of Toussaint L'Ouverture, who had led the slave revolt in Haiti in 1785, and decided the time was ripe for a raid on the arsenal at Harper's Ferry, Virginia. He thought slaves would rise up and follow him in his holy crusade. They didn't, but his subsequent trial and hanging are seen as the sparks that finally set off the great conflagration of the Civil War.

11

Horace Mann, 1796–1859
"Be ashamed to die until you have won some victory for humanity."

On July 1, 1837, the president of the Massachusetts Senate shocked his friends and colleagues by resigning to become the low-paid secretary of the Commonwealth's new Board of Education. Horace Mann, a forty-one-year-old childless widower, also gave up the income from his law practice to take the post he had helped create, a position paying just $1,500 per year.

"My law books are for sale," he wrote to a friend. "I have abandoned jurisprudence, and betaken myself to the larger sphere of mind and morals. Having found the present generation composed of materials almost unmalleable, I am about transferring my efforts to the next. Men are cast-iron; children are wax."

Eleven years later—after affecting great reform in not just Massachusetts' public schools but in schools all around the nation—Mann was elected to replace the recently deceased John Quincy Adams in Congress.

"From the time I accepted the secretaryship in June, 1837, until May, 1848, when I tendered my resignation of it, I labored in this cause an average of not less than fifteen hours a day," he wrote in his final report. "From the beginning to the end of this period I never took a single day for relaxation, and months and months together passed without my withdrawing a single evening to call upon a friend."

While in the Massachusetts Legislature, Mann had championed temperance, the building of a state hospital for the insane, and other humanitarian causes. Later, in Congress, he championed abolition and, in his first speech there, said, "I consider no evil as great as slavery." Public education—"the great equalizer of the conditions of men"—was truly his life's passion however. "Other reforms are remedial," he said. "Education is preventative." His advocacy for tuition-free education for all embroiled him in controversy many times, but no one ever questioned his sincerity.

His parents, Thomas and Rebecca Mann, worked a small rocky farm in the rural town of Franklin in southeast Massachusetts. The Commonwealth was one of three states mandating free public education then, but even in the Bay State it was slipshod at best. The early instruction of Horace and his five siblings consisted of a few weeks of ciphering and reading taught by teenage teachers in a one-room schoolhouse, the lessons squeezed in mid-winter between planting, haying, and harvesting seasons. Mann later described his young instructors as "very good people but very poor teachers," and his childhood of constant work, poverty, and tragedy as "not a happy one."

Mann's father died in 1809 when Horace was thirteen years old. Thomas Mann left the farm to his oldest son, Stanley. The other children received a bequest of just $200 each. Horace truly became a self-made Mann—he tutored his little sister Lydia to save the family money and braided straw for hats to make cash. He read *The Pilgrim's Progress* and other books that had been furnished to the town's lending library by Benjamin Franklin. The town's founders, when honoring the great statesman by taking his name in 1778, had asked Franklin for a church bell. Franklin, however, responded that any community named after him should have more regard for "sense than sound," and sent five hundred books instead.

Horace Mann

Thirteen months after Thomas Mann died, Horace's seventeen-year-old brother Stephen, whom he adored, skipped church one Sunday to go swimming and drowned. The town's Congregational minister, the Reverend Nathaniel Emmons, instead of comforting the family, used Stephen's death as the basis for a sermon about dying in the state of sin. Years later, Horace Mann could still recall his beloved, grief-stricken mother's horrified gasps as the minister railed.

"Dr. Emmons preached . . . that even then Stephen might be in eternal torment," biographer George Allen Hubbell wrote in 1910. "In the breast of Horace Mann there raged a tumult of emotions which no words can describe. He went out from that house with a broken heart, his faith in God and in man shattered. . . . He was hurt too deep for tears. He doubted the goodness of a God who could not only take the life of his brother, but was willing to condemn him to everlasting punishment."

Mann would later write, "I feel constantly, and more and more deeply, what an unspeakable calamity a Calvinistic education is. What a dreadful thing it was for me!"

As a teen, Mann continued to work on the family farm and study on his own. When he was twenty, a traveling schoolmaster named Samuel Barrett convinced Mann to try for admission to Brown University in nearby Providence, Rhode Island. Mann studied Latin so intensely for the next six months that he made himself sick, but he passed the entrance exam, entered Brown as a sophomore in 1816 and three years later graduated at the top of his class. His valedictory address was "The Progressive Character of the Human Race," a theme that would guide his life. After graduating, he taught Latin and Greek at Brown and lived with the school's president Asa Messer and his family, including Messer's ten-year-old daughter, Charlotte.

Mann then attended a law school in Litchfield, Connecticut, where "he ranked as the best whist player and the best lawyer at the institution," according to Albert E. Winship, author of 1896's *Horace Mann: The Educator*. In 1823, Mann became a lawyer in Dedham. He won four of every five cases he tried, but made far less money than he could have.

"It was a financial misfortune that he would never try a case in which he did not believe he was in the right," Winship wrote.

During that time, Mann also became active in Whig party politics and in social causes, and he became an eloquent public speaker. The people of Dedham elected him their state representative in 1827.

In 1829, the tall and lanky thirty-two-year-old Mann sent a letter to Charlotte Messer, now age twenty: "In obedience to feelings whose utterance I can no longer repress, I take the liberty of this mode to request permission to visit you hereafter in the character of an avowed, as I hitherto have done in that of a secret admirer."

They married in September 1830. The young idealistic legislator and his pretty bride with a "holy and beautiful nature" set up their household in Dedham. Years later, Mann wrote, "During that period . . . for me, there was a light upon earth brighter than any light of the sun, and a voice sweeter than any of nature's harmonies."

Less than two years after their nuptials, Charlotte sickened with tuberculosis and died. If the death of his father and favorite brother had changed Horace Mann, the death of his young wife almost killed him. Mann's hair turned white overnight and he resigned his seat in the House. "I seem to stand in a world of shadows," he wrote. "That which gave light and beauty and reality to all is gone." His friends, alarmed by his depression, urged him to move to a Boston boarding house to be near people. He did, but was soon plunged into debt trying to pay off notes he had cosigned for his brother Stanley, who abandoned his family and farm and disappeared to Kentucky. For the next three years, the grief-stricken Mann often slept in his law office to save on rent and skipped eating dinner because he was so broke.

His tragedy and hardships did not make Mann's heart harden however. He increasingly devoted himself to humanitarian causes in the state Senate, to which he was elected in 1834. He became friends with Dr. Samuel G. Howe, first director of the Perkins School for the Blind, Unitarian preacher William Ellery Channing, abolitionist politician Charles Sumner, and schoolteacher Dorothea Dix, who would soon take up the cause of the insane.

Mann had also long been intrigued by the work of James G. Carter, a legislator from Leominster, who had written an 1824 report calling for education reform in Massachusetts. Carter had sponsored an 1827 bill to establish state "normal schools" to train teachers and a state Board of Education, but it failed to pass the House by one vote.

Massachusetts had legislated free public education since colonial days. In 1647, the colony's General Court passed the "Old Deluder" Act, which said: "It being one chief object of that old deluder, Satan, to keep men from the knowledge of the Scriptures . . ." mandated any town with more than fifty households to appoint a teacher and provide a school. The system had fallen into disrepair by the nineteenth century though. One-room schoolhouses like the one Mann had attended existed all over Massachusetts, but they were poorly funded and almost all were open only in the winter. The majority of the teachers had no training and worked other jobs most of the year. Many towns closed their schools because unruly boys beat up the teachers, who were often younger than they were. Carter had discovered at least one third of the children in Massachusetts did not attend school at all.

"Many [teachers] were incompetent; their only method of instruction was to compel memorization through fear of physical punishment," according to the book, *Horace Mann Centennial: 1837–1937,* published by the Massachusetts Department of Education. "Because of this low status of education in the public schools, leading citizens in many communities established private schools and academies for the training of their children. This in turn brought about even greater neglect of the common school."

Mann, already convinced that free public education could cure society's ills, wholeheartedly joined Carter's cause when he returned to politics. Carter's bill, "An Act Relating to Common Schools," finally passed in 1837. It established a State Board of Education and mandated the appointment of a secretary to be "reasonably compensated." Mann, as president of the Massachusetts Senate, signed the bill on April 19, 1837, and was one of eight men appointed to the board by Governor Edward Everett. On June 29, much to the disappointment of Carter's supporters, the board elected Mann the Commonwealth's first Secretary of Education. He took the position—although it only paid half of the $3,000 he earned annually as a senator and far less than what he could earn in his law practice—with much awe and trepidation.

"What a thought to have the future minds of such multitudes dependent in any perceptible degree upon one's own exertions," he wrote. "It is such a thought as must mightedly energize or totally overwhelm any mind that can comprehend it. . . . Few undertakings according to my appreciation of it have been greater. I know of none which may be more fruitful in beneficent results. God grant me an annihilation of selfishness, a mind of wisdom, a heart of benevolence."

Still grieving the death of Charlotte, Mann threw himself into the cause of free public education with an almost religious fervor. He visited towns and districts throughout the Commonwealth in his first year as secretary to assess the schools and found most greatly lacking. He spoke with passion on the need to support public education everywhere he went, often to small audiences, but he refused to be discouraged. He wrote an annual report that—along with the *Common School Journal* he founded and edited—laid out his planned reforms and his effort to standardize education. In his first annual report, Mann wrote, "Teaching is the most difficult of all arts and the profoundest of all sciences." The board soon established three normal schools for teacher training in Lexington, Barre, and Bridgewater. The normal school in Lexington, which opened on July 3, 1839, was the first in the country and later became Framingham State College.

Working tirelessly, Mann became embroiled in numerous controversies—including one over which books should be used in every school, one over the education of the children of Irish immigrants, and another over the use of corporal punishment.

The book controversy and his support of nonsectarian public education pitted Mann, a liberal Unitarian, against evangelical Congregational and Baptist ministers. Mann believed each school should have a library of forty core books to lend to students and their families. When Mann—who wanted the books to reflect ethical principles common across Protestantism—rejected the fire and brimstone books of several powerful fundamentalist ministers for inclusion, they accused him of being anti-religion. Others accused Mann of being anti-Catholic and criticized his belief in phrenology, a pseudo-science widely popular in the early nineteenth century that held people's character could be determined by the contours and bumps on their skulls.

Mann also caught flak from two sides in the immigrant controversy. Even before the great potato famine of 1846–1849 drove tens of thousands of Irish immigrants to Massachusetts, many poor Irish families had come to work on railroads. Mann saw hundreds of Irish children living in squatters' camps, and pushed for laws requiring towns to provide schooling for them, even though they were not permanent residents. Property owners whose taxes supported the schools were opposed to those laws, as were many of the immigrants who wanted their children to work and who called truant officers "kidnappers."

Mann slowly won both groups to his cause by elucidating the benefits of public education for all of society.

"Every wise, humane measure adopted for [the immigrants'] welfare, directly promotes our own security," he wrote in the *Common School Journal*. "The children of this people will soon possess the rights of men, whether they possess the characters of men or not."

In 1839, Democrat Marcus Morton won the governorship from Everett by a single vote. Morton and his allies in the legislature tried to abolish the normal schools and the State Board of Education but their bill failed in the House. Morton's successor, Whig John Davis, again tried to abolish the board in 1840 and also failed, although that vote was so close that it left Mann shaken. Since some of the board's opponents in both cases cited the expense, as the country was still reeling from a depression caused by the Panic of 1837, Mann decided to focus on public education's role in regaining economic prosperity.

"Education is not only a moral renovator and multiplier of intellectual powers . . . but the surest means of amassing property," he wrote in his Fifth Annual Report.

Mann's disdain for corporal punishment caused another controversy and a war of words with thirty-one Boston schoolmasters. "It is a sad exchange, if the very blows, which beat arithmetic and grammar into a boy, should beat confidence and manliness out of him," Mann wrote.

In 1843, Mann wed Mary Peabody, the youngest of the three Peabody sisters well known in Boston literary and reform circles. Mary's sister Sophia had married writer Nathaniel Hawthorne just months earlier. The Manns honeymooned in Europe so they could visit schools there and meet with Charles Dickens and other reformers. Mann wrote his Seventh Annual Report on the ship on the way back and praised European, particularly German, schools so much that he was accused of being anti-American.

The Manns' marriage was a happy one and Mary Peabody Mann gave birth to three sons even as she continued her own career in writing and education.

By 1845, common schools had spread across the country and Horace Mann, espousing, "the absolute right of every human being who comes into this world to an education," had become a celebrated national figure. In his Ninth Annual Report he wrote, "The common school is the greatest discovery ever made by man."

By then, Mann had garnered support from all classes in the Bay State. Businessmen believed Mann's theory that public education would lessen the chances of their greatest fear—mob rule and disruption of commerce. Immigrants and the native working class, while competing for jobs, saw education as a way for their families to prosper, and stopped balking at the minimum six-month school term and compulsory attendance Mann established. His reforms were supported with donations from industry leaders and by the legislature—by 1848, Massachusetts had spent more than $2 million on school buildings and equipment, and established fifty new public high schools. Teachers' salaries had more than doubled.

That same year, John Quincy Adams, who had returned to the Congress after serving as president—still the only former president to do so—collapsed on the floor of the House of Representatives from a stroke and died two days later. Mann was elected to replace him.

While in Congress, Mann carried on Adams's anti-slavery work. He advocated for immediate abolition even though it might mean war. "Interference with slavery will excite civil commotion in the South," he wrote. "But it is best to interfere. Now is the time to see whether the Union is a rope of sand or a band of steel."

Mann volunteered as pro bono legal counsel for two men who had been indicted for trying to free seventy-six slaves in Washington, D.C. He even gave editorial advice to Harriet Beecher Stowe, who upon finishing her nation-changing book, *Uncle Tom's Cabin*, in 1852, sent Mann a letter saying, "In the close of it I think you may trace the result of some of your suggestions." In 1850, Mann became involved in a huge controversy with U.S. senator Daniel Webster over the fugitive slave law, which abolitionists found odious but Webster supported as a compromise to save the Union. Mann responded by calling his fellow Bay State legislator, "a fallen star! Lucifer descending from Heaven!" Webster's supporters subsequently blocked Mann's nomination for re-election as a Whig later that year, but he ran as an independent anti-slavery candidate and won.

In 1852, Mann was nominated to run for governor by the Massachusetts Free Soil party but he lost the election. He then accepted an offer to become the first president of Antioch College, a liberal Protestant co-ed school in Ohio. During his time there, he saved the college from bankruptcy by forming a syndicate of New England investors, but the constant work of raising money took so much out of him that he became ill.

The "Father of American Public Schools" died from cancer on August 2, 1859. He delivered his last public address at the Antioch College commencement just two months earlier.

"I beseech you to treasure up in your hearts these my parting words," he told the graduates. "Be ashamed to die until you have won some victory for humanity."

12

Dorothea Lynde Dix, 1802–1887
The Voice for the Mad

On March 28, 1841, Dorothea Lynde Dix, a prim Boston schoolteacher one week shy of her thirty-ninth birthday, volunteered to lead a Sunday school lesson for female inmates in the East Cambridge House of Correction.

When she finished the lesson, she took what would prove to be a world-changing walk through the jail.

Over the jailer's objections, Dix, still weak from a recent battle with tuberculosis and depression, boldly climbed down the stairs into the lower level, where insane inmates were packed into dark unheated dungeons, some chained to walls or sleeping on the cold stone floor, some naked, all filthy and underfed.

Their only "crime," she would later write, was that they were mentally ill.

In the early 1800s, most Americans believed "maniacs, lunatics, idiots, and madmen" were less than human, and that they could not appreciate cleanliness or even feel extremes in temperature. The insane from well-to-do families were locked up at home or in private asylums dedicated to "moral treatment." They were the lucky ones. Few public asylums existed. Most communities in the United States had almshouses or poorhouses where orphans, the indigent, and the mentally ill were all lumped together. Many towns and counties would

Dorothea Lynde Dix

actually auction off their insane paupers—winning bidders would then put their strong bodies and weak minds to work at the most menial and repetitive tasks.

The insane were also often imprisoned, locked up with criminals, and whipped and abused by cruel jailers for not following orders they couldn't even understand. Prisons around the country created a revenue stream by charging admission fees. For 25 cents, visitors could tour prisons to view the criminals behind bars and to laugh at the antics of the insane, much like children being amused by chimpanzees at a zoo today.

Few believed that treatment was wrong. Dix, however, was horrified by what she saw that day in Cambridge. "If I am cold, they are cold; if I am weary, they are distressed; if I am alone, they are abandoned," she would later write.

When Dix protested to the jailer that the dungeons had no heat, he shrugged and replied that insane people did not feel the cold—after all, they often tore their clothes off—and they would not be safe with stoves in their rooms anyway. Dix went to the East Cambridge court and demanded the cells be heated, and the court agreed. That victory sent Dorothea Dix on a mission that would consume the rest of her life.

"It was thus that, in the East Cambridge jail, Miss Dix was first brought into immediate contact with the overcrowding, the filth, and the herding together of innocent, guilty, and insane persons, which at that time characterized the prisons of Massachusetts, and the inevitable evils of which were repeated in even worse shape in the almshouses," wrote biographer Francis Tiffany in her 1890 book, *The Life of Dorothea Lynde Dix*.

Throughout the 1840s and 1850s, Dix would spend virtually her every waking minute reforming prisons and the way the insane were treated in America and beyond. In 1843, only 13 public hospitals for the insane existed in the United States. By 1850, there were 123 and Dix helped found 32 of them directly. She became the symbol of reform in the treatment of the insane—John Greenleaf Whittier wrote her letters of admiration and his fellow poet, Worcester native Elizabeth

Bishop, would later write, "the only prose book I ever thought I wanted to write is a book about the life of Dorothea Dix."

That life began in Hampden, Maine, then a frontier of Massachusetts, on April 4, 1802. Dorothea was the oldest of Joseph and Mary Dix's three children. Her grandfather, Dr. Elijah Dix, a wealthy physician from Worcester, was a patriot and an honorable man. At the outbreak of the Revolutionary War, his loyalist partner, Dr. Sylvester Gardiner, had fled to England. At the end of the war, Dr. Dix sailed across the Atlantic to pay Gardiner for his share of the practice, even though wartime legislation had canceled the debt.

Dr. Dix moved to Boston and opened a pharmacy, but he made his real fortune by speculating on twenty thousand acres of timberland in Maine. The towns of Dixfield and Dixmont were named for him there. He died when Dorothea was seven.

"He stood out as the one bright spot in her earliest memories, implanting in her mind a life-long admiration for his robust and picturesque qualities," Tiffany wrote. "Indeed, of the many great asylums for the insane which she was later instrumental in founding, the only one she ever permitted to be associated with her own name was Dixmont Hospital in Pennsylvania, a concealed tribute to her grandfather, as founder of the town of Dixmont, Maine."

In sharp contrast to her hard-working and resourceful grandfather, Dorothea's father was an alcoholic ne'er-do-well and her listless mother suffered from depression. Before the British sailed up the Penobscot River and occupied Hampden during the War of 1812, the Dix family fled to Barnard, Vermont, where Mary presided over a grim and cheerless household. Joseph became an itinerant Methodist preacher and was seldom home. From the time she could hold a needle, Dorothea, called Dolly by her family, was forced to stitch together heavy paper religious tracts for her father to sell. Because of her mother's chronic illnesses, she also had to care for her younger brothers. In later life, Dorothea would often lament, "I never knew childhood."

The family moved to Worcester when Dorothea was twelve, but she soon ran away to live with her grandmother in Boston. The aged, wealthy Mrs. Dix could not provide much in the way of mothering, but she did provide Dorothea, already a voracious reader, with some formal schooling. Two years later, when she was just fourteen, Dorothea returned to Worcester to live with a great aunt and to open her own school for younger children. The tall and willowy schoolmarm—she had already reached her adult height of 5-foot-7—would whip misbehaving boys, as was the custom of the day, according to Thomas J. Brown, author of 1998's *Dorothea Dix, New England Reformer*.

"She spared girls the birch rod but devised other severe punishments for them," Brown wrote. "With a fine Puritan appreciation for the power of shame, she compelled one girl to walk during the busy Worcester Court week wearing a large placard that branded her, 'A Very Bad Girl Indeed.'"

In 1821, Dix, then nineteen, returned to Boston and opened a private school for older children. She also ran a free evening school for poor children. She became a devout Unitarian and governess for the children of William Ellery Channing, the influential pastor of the Federal Street Church in Boston. Channing's doctrine, "Man must be sacred in man's sight," became a guiding influence on her life.

Dix also wrote several books for children over the next decade, including, in 1824, the phenomenally successful *Conversations on Common Things*, an encyclopedia that answered questions such as, "Why do we call this month January?" and "Does cinnamon grow on trees?" She became infatuated with Edward Bangs, an older distant cousin, but after that brief romance ended she never had a serious relationship again. Much like her mother, Dorothea suffered from ill health throughout her life. In 1836, she became so sick with tuberculosis and depression that she closed her school and took a trip to Europe, where she planned to recuperate in the Italian sunshine. She never made it to Italy, though, because she collapsed again upon her arrival in England. While recuperating there and staying with friends of the Channing family, she met reformers interested in changing the way the insane in England were treated. Although the 1820s and 1830s were decades of great reform in America, no one in the States had yet tackled the problems of the mentally ill.

Her mother and grandmother both died while Dix was in England. When she returned in 1837, she found she had inherited enough money so that, combined with royalties from her books—*Conversations* eventually went through sixty editions—she would never have to work again. She was still too weak to reopen her school, so she rested and did some traveling. She immersed herself in the church, in her close female friendships, and in writing poetry and letters.

"From an early age, Dorothea avoided frivolity in attire, preferring dark, simple dresses and wearing her hair parted down the middle of her head and stretched across her ears to a tight knot in back," Elisabeth Lasch-Quinn wrote in 1997's *Against the Tide.* "In her nature there lodged an intensity, a search for perfection, an awful seriousness, dwelling there side by side with an unyielding reserve, that made for a deportment considered old-fashioned, ultra-ladylike, even in those days of gentle manners."

In March of 1841, Dix accepted the fateful invitation from a ministerial student to teach Sunday school at the East Cambridge lockup. Her shock and horror at what she saw gave her life new meaning. She impressed upon reformer and abolitionist Charles Sumner (who was later caned on the U.S. Senate floor by a supporter of slavery) and Dr. Samuel G. Howe, director of the Perkins School for the Blind, to visit the jail themselves. Howe then wrote an article for the *Boston Daily Advertiser* deploring the treatment of the insane there. His piece was fiercely attacked as untrue, but Sumner then penned a letter supporting the doctor.

My dear Howe, I am sorry to say that your article does present a true picture of the condition in which we found those unfortunates.

They were cramped together in rooms poorly ventilated and noi-
some with filth. . . . You cannot forget the small room in which
were confined the raving maniac, from whom long since reason
had fled, never to return, and that interesting young woman, whose
mind was so slightly obscured that it seemed as if, in a moment,
even while we were looking on, the cloud would pass away. In two
cages or pens constructed of planks, within the four stone walls of
the same room, these two persons had spent several months. The
whole prison echoed with the blasphemies of the poor old woman,
while her young and gentle fellow in suffering, doomed to pass her
days and nights in such close connection with her, seemed to shrink
from her words as from blows. And well she might; for they were
words not to be heard by any woman in whom reason had left any
vestige of its former presence. It was a punishment by a cruel man
in heathen days to tie the living to the dead, hardly less horrid was
this scene in the prison at Cambridge.

Unburdened by financial pressures, and buoyed by her
alliance with Sumner and Howe, and by her victory in getting
the lower cells heated in Cambridge, Dix decided to become
"the voice for the mad" and investigate the way the insane were
treated throughout the Commonwealth. Jailers and poorhouse
managers sometimes tried to prevent Dix from visiting, but
she would not be put off.

"Notebook in hand, she started out on her voyage of
exploration, visiting every jail and almshouse from Berkshire
on the west to Cape Cod on the east," Tiffany wrote. "Steadily
accumulating her statistics of outrage and misery, she at last got
together a mass of eye-witness testimony appalling in extent
and detail."

Her investigation took her two years. Dix then compiled
a "memorial," a thirty-two-page report which she signed "D.L.
Dix" and gave to Howe to read to the state legislature.

"I shall be obliged to speak with great plainness, and
to reveal many things revolting to the taste, and from which
my woman's nature shrinks with peculiar sensitiveness," she

wrote. "But truth is the highest consideration. . . . The condition of human beings reduced to the extremest state of degradation and misery cannot be exhibited in softened language, or adorn a polished page. I proceed, gentlemen, briefly to call your attention to the present state of insane persons confined within this Commonwealth, in cages, closets, cellars, stalls, pens; chained, naked, beaten with rods, and lashed into obedience! . . . I beg, I implore you. I demand pity and protection for these of my suffering, outraged sex. . . . Gentlemen, I commit you to a sacred cause!"

Dix's *Memorial to the Legislature of Massachusetts* recounts details of the horrors she found, community by community. In Newburyport, she saw an insane man confined next to a "dead room" filled with corpses. In Westford, she found a naked woman with a chain around her waist securing her to a wall; in Groton, a young man with a chain attached to an iron collar on his neck. In Wayland, she was shown a near-naked wild man in a cage under a woodshed, "fully exposed upon the public road . . . the confinement and cold together had so affected his limbs" that he couldn't stand up.

"Lincoln. A woman in a cage. Medford. One idiotic subject chained, and one in a close stall for 17 years. Pepperell. One often doubly chained, hand and foot. . . . West Bridgewater. Three idiots. Never removed from one room." On page after page, Dix detailed the plight of the mentally ill—penned in cages and in stinking sheds filled with their own excrement, without beds to sleep on, without heat, daylight, or fresh air.

Jailing the insane with felons, she wrote, also did injustice to the convicts who were "doomed day after day and night after night to listen to the ravings of a madman." Dix's sensational memorial was soon reprinted in a pamphlet and excerpted in newspapers.

"Inevitably, a Memorial such as that now described struck and exploded like a bombshell," Tiffany wrote. "'Incredible! Incredible!' was the first natural outcry of humane people. 'Sensational and slanderous lies!' was the swift and fiery rejoinder of selectmen, almshouse keepers, and private citizens in arms for the credit of their towns. Everywhere the newspapers bristled with angry articles."

Despite attacks on her honesty and character, Dix would not be bowed and prevailed upon the legislature to appropriate money needed to restore and expand the Worcester Insane Asylum.

With the single-mindedness of a cat stalking a bird, Dix then began tirelessly traveling around the country by buggy, wagon, stagecoach, steamboat, and railroad, always seeking out powerful and influential allies who believed in her "sacred work." Remember, this was in an era when women seldom traveled alone and their right to vote was still more than seventy years away. In each state, Dix performed the same type of detailed analysis of jails and poorhouses that she had done in Massachusetts. Over the next decade, her detailed and shocking reports were presented in state after state, even in the Deep South where most New England reformers were despised. On a New Orleans steamboat in 1846, she met J. O. King, an Illinois businessman who was part of a group interested in building a public asylum in that state.

"She desired to see for herself the conditions for care of the mentally ill in Illinois," described Frank Norbury, writing in the *Journal of the Illinois Historical Society* in 1999. "Within a week she was out visiting jails and almshouses, including the old Morgan County poorhouse where she found, among other problems, 'a violent insane man . . . confined in a shallow cellar, 12 feet square, with a trap door, under the smoke house, and who was without clothing and straw for his bed and was in a very filthy condition.' With the help of King and his brothers she set out by buggy to seven other counties in Central Illinois and found at least 300 insane persons in the jails and almshouses of these counties. Later she visited some more northerly places, including Galena, and several in the southeastern part of the state."

In 1847, Dix presented her memorial to the Illinois Legislature in which she urged, "Retire not from these halls, in which honor, integrity and justice should rule, until you have rendered this noble service to your fellow citizens."

The lawmakers listened and approved building the Illinois State Hospital. New hospitals for the insane were erected everywhere Dix went, and additions and improvements were made to existing facilities. In the late 1840s, Dix came up with a grand plan. She proposed that a federal land grant of 12.5 million acres be set aside as a public endowment, the income to be used for the benefit of the blind, deaf, mute, and insane. She lobbied Congress from 1848 to 1854. Both branches eventually approved the proposal, but President Millard Fillmore, who favored the act, was replaced in the White House by Franklin Pierce, who vetoed the bill.

(Ironically, Pierce's wife, Jane Appleton Pierce, had already been driven to debilitating mental illness by the death of all three of her children—the last being 11-year-old Ben whose head was crushed in a train wreck in Andover, Massachusetts, a month before Pierce's inauguration. Both parents were unhurt, but forever scarred by witnessing the death of their only surviving child. Jane Appleton Pierce suffered such extreme depression that she spent most of her husband's disastrous single term writing letters to her dead children. She made so few public appearances that she became known as "The Shadow in the White House.")

Discouraged by Pierce's veto, Dix traveled to Europe where she investigated and agitated for reform in fourteen countries. During an audience with Pope Pius IX, she convinced him to improve conditions in a hospital for the insane in Rome. The pope later compared her to Saint Theresa.

When the Civil War began, Abraham Lincoln appointed Dix superintendent of Union army nurses, a duty she performed for the next five years without pay. Her service had mixed results and she was often called "Dragon Dix" because of her autocratic style—she would not, for example, allow attractive women under thirty to serve—and her frequent clashes with the military bureaucracy. "This was not the work I would have my life judged by," she later wrote.

After the war, she continued her labors for the mentally ill, particularly in the southern states where facilities had been neglected or damaged during the hostilities. She finally retired at seventy-nine to a small apartment in the New Jersey State Hospital, the first asylum she had helped plan. By that time, less than 1 percent of the insane in America were in jails, but Dix was greatly discouraged that many of the facilities she had advocated for had become overburdened custodial warehouses instead of the benevolent institutions she envisioned. As her health faded, she continued to write letters supporting mental health reforms but, ever the proper lady, she refused to cooperate on an autobiography.

"My reputation and my services belong to my country," she wrote in a letter. "My history and my affections are consecrated to my friends . . . . giving unnecessary publicity to women while they yet live, and to their works, seems to me singularly at variance with the delicacy and modesty which are the most attractive ornaments of their sex."

Dix was also afraid that an autobiography might influence romantic young women to undertake a mission similar to hers. In the end, she was keenly aware of what she had sacrificed in her long and fruitful, but ultimately lonely, life.

"No, let them fall in love, marry and preside over a happy home," she said. "It will be a thousand times better for them."

Dix died on July 17, 1887.

"Of the numerous reformers of the 19th century, probably none accomplished more than Dorothea Lynde Dix," Harry J. Carman and Harold C. Syrett wrote in their 1952 book, *A History of the American People*. "It would be difficult to point to a greater benefactor of mankind in the 19th-century United States than this frail woman who devoted the vigor of a sound mind to the welfare of unsound ones."

13

Margaret Fuller, 1810–1850
Transcendentalist, Journalist, and Feminist

Margaret Fuller was absolutely brilliant—from her childhood until her untimely death—and she knew it. After meeting Ralph Waldo Emerson in 1836 she declared, "I now know all the people worth knowing in America and I find no intellect comparable to my own."

As an equally confident Dizzy Dean, star pitcher of the St. Louis Cardinals, would say almost a century later, "It ain't bragging if you can back it up," and Margaret Fuller could.

By the time she died at age forty in a shipwreck, Fuller had been an acclaimed teacher and author, a crusading journalist, a literary critic, the first female foreign correspondent for an American newspaper, a mother, a revolutionary in Italy, and, most of all, a great thinker. The 1845 publication of her *Woman in the Nineteenth Century* preceded the first National Convention on Woman's Rights by five years.

Fuller was not particularly praised for her literary prowess, but for her intellect and courage. "It was not what she wrote but what she was that makes her life a vivid influence today," Eleanor Roosevelt said in 1930. Fuller herself once said, "Writing is worthless except as a record of a life."

And what a life. Beginning when she was three, Sarah Margaret Fuller was given daily lessons in mathematics, grammar, history, and classical languages. Her father, Timothy

Margaret Fuller
LIBRARY OF CONGRESS LC-USZ62-47039

Fuller, an intense, Harvard-educated lawyer and four-term United States congressman from Cambridge, drove his oldest child relentlessly. Before she was a teen, she had mastered German and French and had read the classics, including the works of Shakespeare. When she asked for a piano at age ten, her father said he would buy one only if she would practice until she shined.

"To excel in all things should be your constant aim," Timothy Fuller wrote to his daughter. "Mediocrity is obscurity."

Although she later longed for the same love her parents demonstrated for one another, Margaret Fuller would grow to greatly resent her father's rigorous educational methods and the lack of intervention from her mother, Margarett Crane Fuller. Fuller would later attribute her frequently poor health—migraine headaches, nightmares of horses trampling her head, "spectral illusions," and battles with depression—to her formative years.

"Poor child!" she wrote later. "I had no natural childhood."

Fuller's coming to terms with her childhood defined her life in many ways. As the eldest child, she was often called upon to care for her siblings, even into her thirties. When she was five, an ill baby sister died in her arms.

"For the two years following Julia Adelaide's death, Margarett Crane Fuller suffered a period of delicate health," according to Joan Von Mehren, author of 1994's *Minerva and the Muse: A Life of Margaret Fuller*. "Looking back, she remembered how much she enjoyed being with Margaret at this time, taking pleasure in her 'intelligence, rich fancy, buoyant spirits, and extreme activity.' From the first, Margaret's 'superior intelligence, and ready invention' were evident. She loved reading . . . gathering flowers, and 'singing with feeling expression,' and was noticeably adept at imitating unusual sounds. There was one other characteristic that Margaret's mother noticed: 'At this early age she showed great sensitivity to reproof, not so much as tears shed at the time, but silent reserve.'"

Young Sarah Margaret was tall for her age, taking after her mother who, at 5-foot-10, towered over her father. Other children in Cambridge teased her for her height and intelligence. Grade school classmate and future author and physician Oliver Wendell Holmes Sr. recalled years later becoming jealous when Margaret used the word "trite" in a sentence because he did not know what it meant.

When she was nine years old, she sent her father, who spent half of each year in Washington, D.C., a letter:

"I want to ask you a question," she wrote. "Whether my manners ought to increase with my growth or with my years. Mamma says people will judge of me according to my growth. I do not think this is just, for surely our knowledge does not increase because we are tall."

She also asked her father to stop calling her Sarah Margaret. Even though "Sarah" was the name given to her in honor of Timothy's late mother, the precocious schoolgirl wanted to be called just Margaret. Timothy balked, but young Margaret insisted, setting the tone for a willful and unapologetic existence, a fearless journey of exploration that could not be defined by her sex or any other imposed limitations.

"Very early I knew that the only object in life was to grow," she would later write. "I was often false to this knowledge, in idolatries of particular objects, or impatient longings for happiness, but I have never lost sight of it, have always been controlled by it, and this first gift of thought has never been superseded by a later love."

Years later, her confidence, some would call it arrogance, would occasionally drive Emerson and her other Transcendentalist friends to distraction. (Her habit of constantly blinking her eyes also bugged Emerson.) But Margaret Fuller knew early on that she was as smart as any man. Why then, should she act as if she was not?

In 1833, retired from Congress, Timothy Fuller bought a twenty-eight-acre homestead in rural Groton, thirty miles west of Cambridge. He planned to write a biography of Thomas Jefferson while emulating Jefferson's retirement as a farmer-scholar.

"Margaret was appalled at the idea," Margaret Bell wrote in her 1930 book *Margaret Fuller, a Biography*. "Such isolation? How could she live without the friends of Cambridge and the books of Boston?"

Although deeply resentful of the move and depressed by it, Margaret Fuller tried her best to be a good daughter and a responsible eldest child. She determined to make the most of the move by working on her translation of Goethe, the German philosopher she had been intrigued by since childhood, and homeschooling her younger siblings. She also became obsessed with a popular book, *Remarks on the Influence of Mental Cultivation and Mental Excitement on Health*, which connected mental disorders with early intellectual training, convinced that her mood swings and headaches were caused by her intense schooling as a child.

In 1835, she became seriously ill with what her family called "brain fever" and she later said was typhoid fever. She wrote that one night her father came into her room and knelt down beside her bed.

"'My dear, I have been thinking of you in the night, and I cannot remember that you have any faults,'" she recalled her father tenderly saying. "'You have defects, of course, as all mortals have, but I do not know that you have a single fault.' . . . [Those words]—so strange from him who had scarce ever in my presence praised me and who, as I knew, abstained from praise as hurtful to his children—affected me to tears."

A few days later, Timothy Fuller came in from working in the fields. He was ill with Asiatic cholera.

"With the family surrounding him, kissing him and whispering farewells, he died on October 2, 1835," Von Mehren wrote. "Margaret closed his eyes and for the rest of her life held the date in reverence. For years afterward, Margarett Crane Fuller told of 'how Margaret brought the younger children together around the lifeless form of her father, and, kneeling, pledged herself to God that if she had ever been ungrateful or unfilial to her father, she would atone for it by fidelity to her brothers and her sister.'"

Margaret's mourning "worked its way into her psyche, connecting her father's death with all the past losses in her life," Von Mehren wrote. "Sadness and morbidity, as depression was called in her time, became her great enemy and refuge as she struggled with her sense of duty."

Fuller's depression worsened when a planned trip to Europe fell through. A poem she wrote, however, caught the eyes of Ralph and Lydia Emerson, who had moved to neighboring Concord. Friends arranged for her to make an extended—and life changing—visit to their home beginning in July 1836. Emerson later wrote to his brother that he found Margaret's appearance "not prepossessing," but that she was "extraordinary" and great company.

"She studied my tastes, piqued and amused me, challenged frankness by frankness, and did not conceal the good opinion of me she brought with her, nor her wish to please," Emerson wrote. "She was curious to know my opinions and experiences. Of course, it was impossible long to hold out against such urgent assault. She had an incredible variety of anecdotes, and the readiest wit to give an absurd turn to whatever passed; and the eyes, which were so plain at first, soon swam with fun and drolleries, and the very tides of joy and superabundant life."

Emerson introduced Margaret Fuller to Bronson Alcott and other progressive thinkers who would soon make up the Transcendentalists Club. In their company, her brilliant mind and her resentment over her harsh educational upbringing fit perfectly. Emerson, Alcott and the other great thinkers of that group were mostly male, many of them liberal Unitarian ministers. They believed that youngsters—contrary to the Puritan notion that children were "sin defiled" and needed to be harshly drilled and shaped by education—were innocents who learned intuitively and were best taught by drawing out their innate goodness and, through exposure to nature, making them aware of their godliness. Many of the Transcendentalists came to reject all organized religion. Fuller, also a Unitarian, did not, but said, "nowhere I worship less than in places set apart for that purpose. The blue sky seen above the opposite roof preaches better than any brother."

Fuller seized upon the Transcendentalist method of education, employing it while teaching language at Alcott's Temple School in Boston and later at a similarly progressive school in Providence, Rhode Island.

"If we had only been as well brought up in these respects," she wrote of her childhood. "It is not mother's fault that she was ignorant of every physical law, young, untaught country girl as she was; but I can't help mourning, sometimes, that my bodily life should have been so destroyed by the ignorance of *both* my parents."

After two years in Providence, she returned to Boston and launched a celebrated series of "Conversations" for women. For the next five years, her intellect and charisma drew the preeminent female thinkers in the Boston area, including Lydia Emerson, Lydia Parker, and sisters Elizabeth, Mary, and Sophia Peabody. Fuller also became the editor of a new quarterly Transcendentalist journal, *The Dial,* which included essays by Emerson, Henry David Thoreau, George and Sophia Ripley, Alcott, and Elizabeth Peabody.

In 1843 she took a trip with friends to the Great Lakes and was appalled by what white men and alcohol had done to the once proud Native Americans in the Midwest.

"Yes! slave-drivers and Indian traders are called Christians, and the Indian is to be deemed less like the Son of Mary than they!" she wrote in her 1844 book *Summer on the Lakes.* "Wonderful is the deceit of man's heart!"

Also in 1843, after Emerson took over as editor, *The Dial* published Fuller's groundbreaking essay, "The Great Lawsuit: Man versus Men and Woman versus Women," which she later expanded into a book, *Woman in the Nineteenth Century,* published two years later. Upon completion of the book, she said she felt "a delightful glow as if I had put a good deal of my true life in it, as if, suppose I went away now, the measure of my footprint would be left on the earth."

Those words would prove sadly prophetic.

Woman in the Nineteenth Century includes allusions to classic literature, poetic references, and Latin phrases. "To us today much of what she said and wrote seems pedantic and the language, which was that of the scholar of her day, smacks somewhat of the Blue Stocking," Eleanor Roosevelt wrote in the introduction of Bell's *Margaret Fuller, a Biography.* "But all through there is the strain of indomitable courage and fineness of spirit, which is as exhilarating and valuable to us today as it was to those who actually met and knew her."

Stilted literary devices aside, Fuller clearly laid out in plain English in her preface that her goal in writing *Woman in* the *Nineteenth Century* was for women to be accepted as equal partners with men in "the holy work that is to make the earth a part of heaven."

> *My highest wish is that this truth should be distinctly and rationally apprehended, and the conditions of life and freedom recognized as the same for the daughters and the sons of time; twin exponents of a divine thought. I solicit a sincere and patient attention from those who open the following pages at all. I solicit of women that they will lay it to heart to ascertain what is for them the liberty of law. It is for this, and not for any, the largest, extension of partial privileges that I seek. I ask them, if interested by these suggestions, to search their own experience and intuitions for better, and fill up with fit materials the trenches that hedge them in. From men I ask a noble and earnest attention to anything that can be offered on this great and still obscure subject, such as I have met from many with whom I stand in private relations. And may truth, unpolluted by prejudice, vanity or selfishness, be granted daily more and more as the due of inheritance, and only valuable conquest for us all!*

Woman in the Nineteenth Century soon became the blueprint of the nascent women's rights movement, although some early reviews were mixed and Fuller said it was not always easy to lift her head "amidst the shower of public squibs and private sneers." In the book, Fuller reasoned that marriage should be "truly a sacrament" and railed that prostitutes working in the cities were the "prey and spoil of men's brute appetites."

"Anger and a derisive incredulity met her plea for the legal and political emancipation of her sex," Faith Chipperfield wrote in her 1957 book, *In Quest of Love: The Life and Death of Margaret Fuller*. "Her cry, 'Let women be sea-captains if they will,' moved reviewers to mirth. 'A contralto voice in literature,' one said, 'deep and rich but neither mellifluous nor clear.' Others had the hardihood to cite the spinster's want of marital experience. 'Her most direct writing is on a subject no virtuous woman can treat justly,' gibed the *Broadway Journal*.

'Woman is nothing but as a wife. No woman is a true woman who is not wife and mother.'"

Other reviewers were more generous. "Although its language is pretty strong, the thoughts it puts forth are so important that we should rejoice to know it read by every man and woman in America," a reviewer for editor William Cullen Bryant's *Evening Post* wrote.

Horace Greeley, the influential editor of the *New York Tribune*, described Fuller as "the most remarkable and in some respects the greatest woman whom America has yet known" after *The Dial* published the original essay.

"If not the clearest and most logical, it was the loftiest and most commanding assertion yet made of the right of Woman to be regarded and treated as an independent, intelligent, rational being, entitled to an equal voice in framing and modifying the laws she is required to obey, and in controlling and disposing of the property she has inherited or aided to acquire," Greeley would later add about *Woman in the Nineteenth Century*. "Hers is the ablest, bravest, broadest assertion yet made of what are termed Woman's Rights."

Greeley had hired Fuller in 1844 to write literary criticism for his newspaper and she moved to New York, where Greeley would joke, "Let them be sea captains" whenever Fuller waited for him to hold open a door for her.

Fuller wanted more from being a journalist than just writing reviews. At Greeley's urging, she hit the streets to write about prostitution, racism, poverty, and New York's other social problems.

"I always felt great interest in those trampled in the mud to gratify men's passions and wished I might come naturally into contact with them," she wrote. When it was suggested that "fallen women" were beyond help, she responded, "It is not so. I know my sex better."

While in New York, she visited and wrote about Sing Sing prison, Bellevue's madhouse and penitentiary, and the Bloomingdale Asylum for the Insane. Headlines over her stories in the *Tribune* included "Woman in Poverty," "Prison Discipline," "The Problem of the Blind," "Capital Punishment," and "Appeal for an Asylum for Discharged Woman Convicts."

Fuller lived with Greeley and his wife on their farm and they were amazed by her integrity and generosity.

"Had she come into the gold of California," Greeley said, "her first thought would have been to found a house of refuge for fallen women desirous of returning to ways of Virtue."

Fuller soon grew to relish her celebrity as an influential journalist and author. "Hitherto I have given almost all my energy to personal relations," she wrote to her brother Richard. "I no longer feel inclined to this. I wish to share and help impel the general stream of thought."

Fuller did, however, embark on a new personal relationship. At the Greeleys' farm, she met James Nathan, a moody young Jewish German salesman who wanted to be a writer. She was immediately smitten and didn't wait for him to make a move.

"Dear Mr. Nathan," she wrote. "I have long had a presentiment that I should meet intimately one of your race, but I did not expect so civilized an apparition—and with blue eyes!"

The romance was stormy and short lived. In 1846, Fuller sailed to Europe on assignment for the *Tribune,* becoming America's first female foreign correspondent.

Fuller's fame preceded her to the continent and, in Paris and London, she was welcomed as an equal by European intellectuals and artists, including Thomas Carlyle, William Wordsworth, George Sand, Chopin, and Giuseppe Mazzini, the leader of the Italian Unification Movement.

She went to Italy in 1847 and fell in love with Giovanni Angelo Ossoli, a rebel from an impoverished noble family who was ten years younger than her and decidedly not an intellectual. In 1848, Margaret gave birth to their son, Angelo. While Ossoli fought to free Italy from papal influence, Fuller directed a field hospital for the rebels in Rome and continued to send dispatches to the *Tribune.*

"During the siege of Rome, I could not see my little boy," she wrote in a letter home. "What I endured at that time, in various ways, not many would survive. In the burning sun, I went, every day, to wait in the crowd for letters about him. Often they did not come. I saw blood that had streamed on the wall where Ossoli was. I have a piece of the bomb that burst close to him. I sought solace in tending the suffering men; but when I beheld the beautiful, fair young men bleeding to death, or mutilated for life, I felt the woe of all the mothers who had nursed each to that full flower, to see them thus cut down."

The Roman Republic was proclaimed in February 1849 but French forces restored the pope five months later. For safety, Giovanni, Margaret, and Angelo moved from Rome to Florence, where Margaret wrote a history of the Italian Revolution despite constant police surveillance and a lack of money.

In May 1850, the Fuller-Ossolis sailed on the *Elizabeth* for the United States. Early in the voyage, the captain of the ship died from smallpox. Angelo also sickened but recovered. On July 19, the ship crashed into a sandbar one hundred yards off New York's Fire Island during a hurricane. Because of the storm, no rescue effort could be immediately made and twelve hours later, the ship broke up. Crewmembers who survived described those final hours as a watery hell and Margaret's final moments, in which she refused to save herself without the baby and her husband, as heroic. Angelo's body later washed ashore but the bodies of Margaret and Giovanni were never recovered.

Emerson sent Thoreau to New York to walk the beaches and search for Fuller's unfinished manuscript and her papers, but they, too, were never found. In his eulogy for Margaret, Emerson wrote, "If nature availed in America to give birth to many such as she, freedom and honour and letters and art too were safe in this new world."

Three months later, delegates to the first national Woman's Rights Convention in Worcester observed a moment of silence for Fuller. The president of the convention, Paulina

Wright Davis, later revealed that when she heard Fuller planned to return to the United States, she had written to her in hopes that Margaret would attend the convention and take on "the leadership of this movement."

In 1881, thirty-one years after Fuller's death, Elizabeth Cady Stanton and Susan B. Anthony wrote in the *History of Woman Suffrage* that Fuller "possessed more influence on the thought of American women than any woman previous to her time."

14

Elihu Burritt, 1810–1879
The Learned Blacksmith

Early on in the depression of 1837, Elihu Burritt closed the doors of his grocery store for the last time and walked from Connecticut to Massachusetts—and into history.

The slender twenty-six-year-old blacksmith—the grocery store had been a short-term venture—first walked north 115 miles from his hometown of New Britain to Boston, hoping to get a job on a ship. But once there, Burritt heard about the American Antiquarian Society Library in Worcester. He turned west and walked forty more miles.

In Worcester he found the library, a job, a new home—and his destiny.

Before he died, the self-taught Burritt would become fluent in at least fifty languages. More importantly, he would form the League of Universal Brotherhood with tens of thousands of subscribers in America and Europe, and become "the country's greatest man of peace," according to Devere Allen, author of 1930's *The Fight for Peace*.

Henry Wadsworth Longfellow probably modeled his poem "The Village Blacksmith" on Burritt, whom he befriended. Burritt so loved his work with anvil and forge that he turned down a full scholarship to Harvard offered by Longfellow and others so he could continue to bang out horseshoes and study on his own.

Elihu Burritt

"No such person could have lived; and yet he did," Allen wrote. "Consider this man. He was the son of a humble shoemaker; he fraternized with the greatest personages of Europe, who admired him greatly . . . . He is one of our country's greatest figures; he is unknown to the general public."

Burritt was born on December 8, 1810, the youngest of ten children in a poor family—his father was a Revolutionary War veteran, a shoemaker and farmer. His dad died when Elihu was fourteen and Burritt left school a year later to become a blacksmith's apprentice. Three years later, his older brother, Elijah, who had become a respected educator and author of a textbook on astronomy, took him under his wing, and young Elihu took three months off from the forge to attend his brother's school. The world opened up to him there. He displayed great skill in arithmetic, but even more ability in foreign languages. He returned to his job but continued to learn. By night he studied and by day too—Burritt would prop books open on his forge as he worked—and he soon mastered Latin, French, Greek, Spanish, Hebrew, German, and Italian.

Never married, Elihu worked up to fourteen hours a day at the forge—for his entire life he would champion hard physical labor—and then spent his evenings translating Homer's *Iliad* and other classics line by line.

After attending Elijah's school and working and studying on his own in New Haven, Elihu briefly became a teacher. He found however that if he didn't do hard physical work and breathe fresh air, he became sickly. He took a job as a traveling salesman for a short while and then opened a grocery store. When the crash of 1837 came, he decided to get a job on a ship and travel the world so that he could immerse himself in other languages. Penniless, he walked to Boston. Upon reaching the Hub, he heard about the American Antiquarian Society's library in Worcester. Founded by Isaiah Thomas, the library contains millions of books and periodicals, many in foreign languages.

So, Elihu Burritt started walking again. He found a job at William Wheeler's smithy on Union Street in Worcester.

After work each day, he'd go to the American Antiquarian Society's Library and pore over the books, magazines, and newspapers—"such a collection of ancient, modern and Oriental languages that I never before conceived to be collected in one place," he later wrote.

When the library closed for the evening, he would go home to his apartment on Chatham Street and continue studying into the wee hours. By the time he turned thirty, he could read and translate fifty languages. His diary from his first year in Worcester reveals a man driven by an unquenchable intellectual thirst:

"June 18. Headache; forty pages Cuvier's *Theory of the Earth*; sixty-four pages French; eleven hours' forging. *June 19.* Sixty lines Hebrew; thirty pages French; ten pages Cuvier's *Theory*; eight lines Syriac; ten lines Danish; ten ditto Bohemian; nine ditto of Polish; fifteen names of stars; ten hours' forging. *June 20.* Twenty-five lines Hebrew; eight of Syriac; eleven hours' forging. *June 21.* Fifty-five lines Hebrew; eight of Syriac; eleven hours' forging. *June 22.* Unwell; twelve hours' forging."

In 1839, Burritt began editing and publishing a monthly magazine, *The Literary Geminae,* but it failed in less than twelve months, costing him $600 of the $1,000 he had earned as a blacksmith that year. Needing cash, and confident of his ability in languages, Burritt wrote a letter to prominent Worcester publisher William Lincoln, telling him of his background and asking for a part-time job translating books. Lincoln, a well-connected brother of former governor Levi Lincoln Jr., was so impressed by Burritt's story that he sent the letter on to Governor Edward Everett, himself an accomplished linguist. Everett was also impressed and soon spoke about "the Learned Blacksmith" in a speech at the Teacher's Institute in Taunton. Burritt, who had always been so shy and modest that he couldn't look a schoolgirl in the face, was "horrified and astounded" when he read his new nickname in a newspaper account of the speech.

"Governor Everett invited the blacksmith to dinner, and, on behalf of several men of wealth, offered him all the advantages for further study which Harvard University afforded" according to Merle Curti, author of *The Learned Blacksmith: The Letters and Journals of Elihu Burritt*. "Longfellow generously suggested that he would be glad to aid him in every way during his proposed residence at Cambridge. Burritt chose, however, to continue his linguistic work in combination with manual labor, and without teachers. Hard toil he regarded as indispensable to health and happiness, and he had no desire to take flight in the secluded life of a scholar."

In a gracious letter, Burritt told Longfellow, who taught foreign languages at Harvard, that "I feel much attached to Worcester, and it would seem like leaving the best home I have," and that, in any case, he preferred "to stand in the ranks of the workingmen of New England, and beckon them onward and upward . . . to the full stature of intellectual men."

In the meantime, the press—employing "the Learned Blacksmith" nickname—created a celebrity.

"Burritt was a marked man," Allen wrote. "Invitations to lecture poured in upon him; phrenological journals went into ecstasies over his deep-set eyes and bulging brows [Note: Phrenology was a rage in that era—many believed you could learn a lot about a man's character by the contours of his skull]. . . . Fame and fortune now seemed the lot of 'the learned blacksmith.' A career of ease and elegance might readily have been his. But his curious mind forbade it."

Forbade it, because Burritt had been moved by the message in one of the books he had read. He decided one night that Cuvier's *Theory of the Earth* held a singular great truth—nations needed to cooperate instead of fight, and the true destiny of man could only be achieved by a world at peace.

"From that night onward, Elihu Burritt's hand was against the world as it was," Allen wrote. "The craftsman who boasted, and not idly, that he could wield more mechanical tools than any other jack-of-all-trades in Kingdom Come, was out to shape the world to his heart's desire."

Burritt hit the lecture circuit. The Lyceum movement—in which speakers would travel a circuit of town halls and other venues—was huge in New England in the 1840s and the Learned Blacksmith became its star. It didn't hurt that he looked like a leading man. A Swedish novelist, Fredrika Bremer, who met Burritt at about that time, described him as "a very tall and strong-limbed man with an unusually lofty forehead, large, beautiful eyes, and predominatingly handsome and strong features—a man who would excite attention in any company whatever, not only for his figure but for the expression of singular mildness and human love which marks his countenance."

Burritt gave his first lecture "The Importance and Necessity of Educating the Mechanics and Working Men of Our Country" in Worcester in 1842. He gave another similarly themed lecture, "Application and Genius," sixty times in 1843 to enthusiastic audiences up and down the Eastern Seaboard, always returning to his beloved forge in his adopted hometown. Proud of his blue collar, he even asked one lecture promoter to abstain from flowery phrases and introduce him simply as "Elihu Burritt of Worcester, Massachusetts."

An avid diarist, on May 23, 1843, Burritt wrote: "Read Arabic and wrote a page on my Peace lecture. This indeed is snail-like progress, but if unremitting it will come to something in the end. I mean to keep up my courage and not give over on account of my poor facility of composition. In the afternoon I forged 5 hoes in 3 hours; spent the evening in my rooms."

His peace lecture did indeed "come to something." When he spoke out against war at the packed Tremont Temple in Boston, the crowd went wild.

"Present were not only members of the *cognoscenti* and the *literati*, but of the *pacifisti*," Allen wrote. "And these were overwhelmed; crowding forward, they claimed him as their own, and theirs he was in truth."

Back in Worcester, he began publication of the *Christian Citizen*, a newspaper dedicated to the moral advancement of the working class, temperance, the abolition of slavery, and the end of war. Its masthead read, "Peace—God hath made of one blood all nations of men" and included a quotation from the Irish rebel and statesman Daniel O'Connell: "Remember no political change is worth a single crime, or above all, a single drop of human blood." Never financially successful, the *Christian Citizen* would almost bankrupt Burritt within six years.

On New Year's Day, 1845, Burritt decided to expend his energies almost exclusively to one cause. "I find my mind is setting with all its sympathies toward the subject of Peace," he wrote in his journal. "I am persuaded that it is reserved to crown the destiny of America, that she shall be the great peace maker in the brotherhood of nations."

In the next two decades, Burritt would hold true to what has sometimes been described as his "militant pacifism." He led a schism in the American Peace Society by rejecting claims by another movement leader, George Beckwith, that the war with Mexico in 1846 was justified because it was a "defensive war."

"There is no disqualifying reason why the Mexican and American soldiers who stabbed at each other's hearts in the streets of Monterey, might not alternately subscribe to the highest article of faith remaining in the Society's creed, and that too with the points of their bayonets newly dipped in human blood," Burritt responded.

Beckwith's side won out, though, and a disappointed Burritt went to Great Britain. He toured the areas of west Ireland most afflicted by the potato famine and sent a stirring appeal back to the *Worcester Spy* and other Massachusetts newspapers for provisions to be sent to the starving victims. The Boston Relief Committee responded by sending a ship full of food to Cork.

"But it was clear to Burritt that all such humanitarian causes could be best promoted by a permanent, international organization," Curti wrote. "It was at Pershore, a country vil-lage, that he formed, in July, 1846, the League of Universal Brotherhood, devoted to the 'elevation of man, as a being, as a brother, irrespective of his country, color, character, or con-dition.'" By 1848, at least twenty-five thousand people in the United States, thirty thousand in England and thousands more in Germany, France, and Holland had signed the League's pledge, which Burritt had written.

Believing all war to be inconsistent with the spirit of Christianity, and destructive of the best interests of mankind, I do hereby pledge myself never to enlist or enter into any army or navy, or to yield any voluntary support or sanction to any war, by whomsoever or for whatsoever proposed, declared or waged. And I do hereby associate myself with all persons, of whatever country, color, or condition, who have signed, or who shall hereafter sign, this pledge, in a League of Universal Brotherhood, whose object shall be, to employ all legitimate and moral means for the abolition of all war, and all the spirit and manifestations of war throughout the world; for the abolition of all restrictions upon international correspondence and friendly intercourse, and of whatever else tends to make enemies of nations, or prevents their fusion into one peaceful brotherhood; for the abolition of all institutions and customs which do not recognize and respect the image of God and a human brother in every man, of whatever clime, color, or condition of humanity.

Even as wars raged in Europe in the late 1840s and 1850s, Burritt continued his campaign for world peace and justice for working people—walking everywhere he could, championing worker's strikes against war, and holding peace congresses in Paris, Brussels, and other cities. He returned to the States for peace congresses and to lobby in Washington for a penny post-age bill—believing that enabling people to send letters cheaply across the Atlantic would promote world brotherhood. He saw the slavery issue drawing the United States inexorably to war and, in a little newspaper he edited, the *Citizen of the World*, he advocated his scheme of "compensated emancipation," which involved the sale of public lands to provide funds to buy slaves their freedom. From 1856 to the outbreak of the war Burritt championed compensated emancipation as a way to avoid conflict.

"One winter, a typical one, he journeyed 10,000 miles, speaking in the largest cities as well as in smaller towns," Curti wrote. "In addition to almost incessant lectures, he conducted an enormous correspondence: in one month he wrote five hundred letters to enlist support . . . but Burritt could not carry the country: he felt that the hysteria which resulted in the South from the John Brown raid closed all avenues to any discussion of a peaceful settlement of the slavery controversy."

Well-known people of influence and intellect on both sides of the Atlantic all knew of Burritt's work. He and abolitionist United States senator Charles Sumner of Massachusetts were great friends. The mayor of Worcester called Burritt, "truly the Apostle of Peace," during a City Hall ceremony honoring him in 1849. In the 1850s, he dined with President Franklin Pierce and met with many of the movers and shakers of his time—including John C. Calhoun, Henry Clay, Victor Hugo, Charles Dickens, and two British prime ministers.

Burritt had many supporters in his opposition to the war with Mexico in 1846. Southern slave-owners and expansionists favored the war, but—in the North especially—the war was unpopular. A young Illinois congressman named Abraham Lincoln saw the war with Mexico as a land grab by President James K. Polk. A young army officer who fought in the war, Ulysses S. Grant, would later describe it as "the most unjust ever waged by a stronger nation against a weaker nation." Henry David Thoreau went to jail rather than pay his war tax and, in 1847, the Massachusetts Legislature voted for a resolution withholding funds. The war with Mexico, according to the Massachusetts resolution, had been "unconstitutionally commenced by the order of the President . . . for the dismemberment of Mexico, and for the conquest of a portion of her territory . . . [with the] object of extending slavery."

Opposing the Civil War in 1861 took far more courage from Burritt. Although a committed abolitionist, he remained steadfast in his opposition to all war. Especially early on, Burritt had few allies—many Northerners believed the preservation of the Union justified hostilities, and many others, including the majority of Quakers, thought the abolition of slavery made the Civil War a holy struggle. "If this war shall put an end to that execrable system, it will be more glorious in history than that of the Revolution," William Lloyd Garrison wrote in his newspaper, the *Liberator*. Some even accused Burritt of Confederate sympathies when he agreed with *New York Tribune* publisher Horace Greeley that it would have been better to let the South secede than to fight.

Burritt decried "the insidious drifting that has carried nearly all our peace friends into the wake of this war" in a letter to an English friend a month after the surrender of Fort Sumter.

"I have felt distressed at my inability to put forth a feather's weight of influence against the war spirit," Burritt wrote. "In the first place no Northern journal would admit an article against the conflict. Indeed a religious paper in Philadelphia was suppressed because it called it an *Unholy War*. . . . The whole people go for a vigorous prosecution of the war, to the bitter end. I have gone as far as I could, without exposing myself to arrest in opposing the war; but I feel powerless and almost alone."

In 1863, Burritt returned to England and walked to the northernmost tip of Scotland. He then wrote a book, *Walk from London to John O'Groats*, filled with poetic descriptions of the scenery and rural life. In 1865, Lincoln appointed Burritt consular agent at Birmingham, England, a post he held until 1869. In that position, he helped emigrants from the United Kingdom get to the United States. Lincoln borrowed from Burritt's compensated emancipation theory to pay off owners of slaves in the border states during the war, and in 1870, Burritt's postal persistence paid off and Congress lowered the cost of sending a transatlantic letter to 6 cents.

Elihu Burritt never saw his vision for world peace fulfilled. The Franco-Prussian War enveloped Europe in 1870 and England's continuous "reign of Satanic devastation" in India distressed Burritt greatly. He returned to the United States in 1871 and spent his final years farming a small plot of land in his native New Britain. In 1872, Yale gave him an honorary degree.

"I feel I am played out as a lecturer," he wrote to a friend in 1874. "I am deeply into my philological work. I have finished the Sanscrit, Hindustan, and Persian series, and am about half through with the Turkish . . . Then I intend to take up the Semitic family, or Arabic, Hebrew, Syriac and Ethiopic . . . Thus you see I am beginning a work which should occupy a long life."

He died five years later and has all but been forgotten.

"We have trouble understanding pacifism because of unfamiliarity," Colman McCarthy, director of the Center for Teaching Peace in Washington, D.C., wrote to the *Boston Globe* in 1983. "In grammar school and high school history courses, our children are told more about the exploits of generals—Grant, Lee, Pershing, MacArthur—than of the conquests of unarmed leaders like Martin Luther King and Gandhi. The textbooks glorify Theodore Roosevelt and his Rough Riders, Stonewall Jackson and Davy Crockett, but peacemakers like Sojourner Truth, Lucretia Mott, Elihu Burritt, Jeanette Rankin, A.J. Muste, William Penn or Thomas Merton do not rate even footnote status. Historical figures who think disputes among nations are best settled by weapons and violence are exalted, while those who think better of humanity—that reason, non-cooperation and organized resistance can stop war—are seen as fools or dreamers."

15

Henry David Thoreau, 1817–1862
"Live deep and suck out all the marrow of life"

Henry David Thoreau spent just one night in jail for refusing to pay a poll tax in protest against slavery and the Mexican War. His essay "Civil Disobedience," which sprang from that night, was published in a magazine that lasted for just one issue.

That one night and that essay changed the world.

"There are thousands who are *in opinion* opposed to slavery and to the war, who yet in effect do nothing to put an end to them," Thoreau wrote, "who, esteeming themselves children of Washington and Franklin, sit down with their hands in their pockets, and say that they know not what to do and do nothing."

A half-century later, Mohandas Ghandi read "Civil Disobedience" and, properly inspired, led decades of nonviolent protest that expelled Britain from India. In America, a century after Thoreau wrote "Civil Disobedience," Martin Luther King Jr. read the essay, and soon began leading nonviolent protests that would force America to address racial inequality and end legalized segregation.

"I became convinced that non-cooperation with evil is as much a moral obligation as is cooperation with good," King wrote. "No other person has been more eloquent and passionate in getting this idea across than Henry David Thoreau."

Henry David Thoreau

Thoreau wasn't just a protestor of slavery and other injustices. Though he died at age forty-four and seldom left his beloved hometown of Concord while he lived, he was one of America's great naturalists, one of the nineteenth century's finest thinkers and most prolific writers. He didn't drink alcohol, smoke tobacco, or eat meat—or shine his shoes. He never voted, never went to church, never married. He hated the invasiveness of trains and the desperation of commerce and industry. He walked everywhere he could. He worked only when he needed money.

"He declined to give up his large ambition of knowledge and action for any narrow craft or profession, aiming at a much more comprehensive calling, the art of living well," his best friend and mentor, Ralph Waldo Emerson, said at Thoreau's funeral. "No truer American existed than Thoreau."

Indeed, Thoreau lived deeply, in touch with the natural world like "an Indian" as one of his other admirers said. He could identify every plant and animal track in the forests and spent as much time as he could outdoors. He was adept with a hoe and a hammer. "Not one man in a million loses so few of the hours of life," his friend William Ellery Channing wrote after Thoreau died. "The hand that wrote *Walden* . . . could build a boat or a house."

Thoreau wrote some of the all-time most quoted sentences: "Under a government which imprisons any unjustly, the true place for a just man is also in prison," and "If a man does not keep pace with his companions, perhaps it is because he hears a different drummer" are just a couple of examples. His explanation of why he built his cabin on the shore of Walden Pond and lived there for twenty-six months has inspired countless readers to "simplify, simplify" their own lives.

"I went to the woods," he wrote, "because I wished to live deliberately, to front only the essential facts of life, and see if I could not learn what it had to teach, and not, when I came to die, discover that I had not lived."

Thoreau's way of living was based not only on nature, but on the principle of obeying his conscious instead of government law. He was surprised when he was arrested for not paying his poll tax, but angered when his aunt paid his fine and he was released. Thoreau then wrote his "Civil Disobedience" essay as a lecture he first delivered at the Concord Lyceum on January 26, 1848. Elizabeth Peabody published it with the headline, "Resistance to Civil Government" in the first and only issue of her *Aesthetic Papers* magazine in May 1849.

By then, Thoreau had already lived in the woods near Walden Pond. That two-year experiment, undertaken to "live deep and suck out all the marrow of life," still exerts a profound effect upon youth and the environmental movement worldwide. His book *Walden* is considered among the most important ever written by an American author. Some of his contemporaries were dubious, however, when Thoreau spoke about his time at the pond in a lecture at Worcester City Hall in 1849.

"His discourse was intended as an autobiography of two years of life in the woods—an experiment by the lecturer to illustrate, not perhaps so much the absurdity of the present organization and customs of society, as the ease with which a man of resolution and stern expedients may have ample leisure for the cultivation of his intellectual powers and the acquisition of knowledge," a *Worcester Palladium* reviewer wrote. "Such philosophers illustrate the absurdities the human mind is capable of. What would a forest of them be good for? . . . They are watches without any pointers; their springs and wheels are well adjusted, and perform good service; but nobody is the wiser for it, as they do not tell the time of day."

During Thoreau's lifetime and even after his death, some agreed with the Worcester reviewer that he was overrated and self-centered, an egoist slacker who filtered everything, even nature, through his own senses. Many others, though, think no writer before or after has had such a profound effect on the world.

"People seldom react to Henry David Thoreau mildly," author Walter Harding, a founding member of the Thoreau

Society, wrote in 1960. "For a century his writings have been a center of controversy, with his partisans ardently hailing him as *the* major American writer and their opponents vehemently denouncing him as a second-rate imitator of Emerson . . . . His contemporaries reacted no less violently to Thoreau as a person than our contemporaries do today to his ideas. In fact, so violently did they react that their descendants in Concord, Massachusetts, his hometown, today—a century later—are still debating his personality as though he were still alive. I know of one dear old lady who once each year makes a pilgrimage to Sleepy Hollow Cemetery in Concord where Thoreau is buried, and there, after laying wreaths of flowers on the nearby graves of Emerson and Hawthorne, turns to Thoreau's grave, and shaking her fist, says, 'None for you, you dirty little atheist.'"

Thoreau was, and always will be, an enigma—America's first great environmentalist who accidentally set the Concord forest on fire, a man who prided himself on living simply in the woods at Walden Pond, but who would sometimes walk to his parents' home nearby for supper, a pacifist who later wrote an eloquent appeal supporting the violent actions of abolitionist John Brown. Boys in Concord loved to join him on his nature walks and hear his stories, but many of his other neighbors in Concord thought Thoreau was just plain weird—an ill-tempered hermit. His friends found him sometimes shy, but also glib and funny. When his first book, *A Week on the Concord and Merrimack Rivers,* sold poorly, the publisher returned most of the first printing to him. "I have now a library of nearly nine hundred volumes," he wrote to a friend, "over seven hundred of which I wrote myself."

Like his father, Thoreau was short of stature and he was also bone-deep ugly. Writer Nathaniel Hawthorne, who became a great friend, remarked on Thoreau's appearance shortly after meeting him in 1842: "He is a singular character—a young man with much of the wild original nature still remaining in him; and so far as he is sophisticated, it is in a way and method of his own," Hawthorne wrote in his notebook. "He is as ugly as sin, long-nosed, queer-mouthed, and with uncouth and somewhat rustic, although courteous manners, corresponding very well with such an exterior. But his ugliness is of an honest and agreeable fashion, and becomes much better than beauty."

Thoreau was born on July 12, 1817, on his maternal grandmother's farm in Concord, the third of four children of John B. Thoreau and his wife Cynthia Dunbar Thoreau. The family moved briefly to nearby Chelmsford and then to Boston, sixteen miles to the east, but soon returned to Concord. There young David Henry (he reversed the two names in the 1830s) grew up with his older brother John and sisters Helen and Sophia—a barefoot boy driving the cows to the pasture and playing on the milldam and around the pond behind it. His family believed in abolition—in the 1830s, Thoreau's mother and sisters were founding members of the Concord Ladies Anti-Slavery Society—and participated as conductors on the Underground Railroad. As a young man, Henry often escorted escaped slaves to the next stop on their ultimate journey to freedom in Canada.

"He was always a thoughtful, serious boy, in advance of his years—wishing to have and do things his own way, and ever fond of wood and field; honest, pure, and good; a treasure to his parents, and a fine example for less happily constituted younglings to follow," Channing wrote in a series of 1860s newspaper articles after interviewing Thoreau's mother. "Thus [his friend] Samuel Hoar gave him the title of 'the judge,' from his gravity; and the boys at the town school used to assemble about him as he sat on the fence, to hear his account of things."

Thoreau attended Concord schools and then Harvard University. In his sophomore year he contracted the tuberculosis he would battle recurrently for the next twenty-seven years. He graduated in 1837 and met writer Ralph Waldo Emerson, fourteen years his senior, and the two became lifelong friends. Thoreau had already read Emerson's *Nature* twice by then, and had heard him speak at Harvard, but even though Emerson had moved in 1835 to Concord, which only had a population of about two thousand, they had never previously met.

"'What are you doing now?' he asked [me]," Thoreau wrote after that first meeting. "'Do you keep a journal?' So I make my first entry today."

Thus began one of the most celebrated writing careers in history—over the next quarter century, Thoreau's journals alone would total twenty-one volumes and two million words. Critic Alfred Kazin would later say that Thoreau needed "to write about his life in order to convince himself that he had lived it."

Emerson introduced Thoreau to the Transcendentalist Club centered in Concord and Boston, which included reformer Theodore Parker, writer Margaret Fuller, educator Bronson Alcott, and many of the other great thinkers of the day. The Transcendentalists rejected the Calvinist notion of original sin and believed that people were born good, blank slates, and that by replacing the pursuit of material gain with a communion with nature they could realize important truths.

After college, Thoreau took a job as the teacher in the Concord public school but quit after two weeks when the superintendent insisted he cane unruly boys. He started working at his father's lead pencil factory behind the family home on Main Street and soon devised a way to produce the best pencils in America. He quickly became bored with pencil making and quit, although he would return to work there from time to time when he needed money.

In 1838, he and his brother John started their own school in Concord. They both fell in love with the same woman, seventeen-year-old Ellen Sewall from Cape Cod, and each—first John and then Henry—proposed to her. She rejected both and Henry never had another romantic interest. His three siblings also never married.

In 1840, the Transcendentalist Club launched a magazine, *The Dial*. The first issue included two essays by Thoreau.

The Thoreau brothers closed their school in 1841 when John became too weak to continue due to his own battles with tuberculosis. Henry then accepted Emerson's offer to live with his family and work for them as a handyman.

Within a year, John contracted lockjaw after a shaving cut became infected and he died in Henry's arms. The brothers, just two years apart in age, had been extremely close—*A Week on the Concord and Merrimack Rivers* is based on an 1839 canoe trip they took together.

"Thoreau was shattered by his brother's death, and in the following days he suffered psychosomatically from symptoms of lockjaw himself," William E. Cain wrote in his 2000 book, *A Historical Guide to Henry David Thoreau.*

Fifteen days after John passed away, the Emerson's five-year-old son Waldo died from scarlet fever. Those two deaths in January 1842 stunned Thoreau and made his path clear. In March, he wrote a letter to his friend Isaiah Williams that said, "All great good is very urgent, and need not be postponed."

Over the next three years, Thoreau worked for the Emersons, wrote, spoke at the Concord Lyceums, briefly moved to Staten Island to tutor Emerson's nephew, and also helped Emerson edit *The Dial*. He became increasingly disenchanted with "progress"—more and more people, especially new immigrants, were working for others—and when the Boston-Fitchburg Railroad noisily and noxiously came to Concord in 1844, he wrote, "We do not ride on the railroad, it rides upon us."

On July 4, 1845, Thoreau moved into a one-room shanty, a fifteen-foot by ten-foot cabin that he had bought from an Irish immigrant and then reassembled on a plot of land Emerson owned on Walden Pond. He furnished it with three chairs, a table, a desk and a small mirror, and in the fall built a fireplace and chimney. He tended a two-and-a-half-acre vegetable garden, rowed his boat, played his flute, walked in the woods, and observed the nature around him. He voraciously read nonfiction. He wrote *A Week on the Concord and Merrimack Rivers* and the first of seven drafts of *Walden*. He sometimes visited his parents and friends in town and often entertained visitors at his cabin. He was arrested for failure to pay his poll tax one day when he walked into Concord and spent that fateful night in jail. Other than that, his time at the pond was interrupted only by a trip to the Maine woods.

"He was at Walden less of a sojourner in nature than he was a maker of books, an indefatigable writer who was always writing," Cain wrote. "He went to Walden Pond to write books and to gather experiences for books. . . . For Thoreau, writing was the fundamental fact of existence, and everything else he made secondary to it; even nature, which he cherished, was in essence raw material for his literary imagination."

After two years, two months, and two days at Walden, Thoreau moved back in with the Emersons. "I left the woods for as good a reason as I went there," he wrote. "Perhaps it seemed to me that I had several more lives to live, and could not spare any more time for that one."

For the next seven years, Thoreau continued to write and rewrite. He later described his writing method as: "Find out as soon as possible what are the best things in your composition, and then shape the rest to fit them." He also worked as a land surveyor, collected plant samples for naturalist Louis Agassiz, and, at Emerson's request, went to Long Island in 1850 to search the beaches for Margaret Fuller's final manuscript after she, her husband, and their son were lost in a shipwreck.

Walden, or, Life in the Woods was published in 1854 and did much better than *A Week on the Concord and Merrimack Rivers* had. With the exception of 1859–1862, *Walden* has never been out of print. Many of the lines in it, such as "the mass of men lead lives of quiet desperation" have become legend.

Thoreau continued to speak and write on the natural world and society in the tumultuous 1850s. He thought the California Gold Rush was a pathetic exercise in greed: "It makes God to be a moneyed gentleman who scatters a handful of pennies in order to see mankind scramble for them," he wrote. "Going to California. It is only three thousand miles nearer to hell."

In his "Slavery in Massachusetts" lecture and essay, he questioned his own life of withdrawal and was bothered by the high ground he gave away while at Walden. "I did not know at first what ailed me," he wrote. "At last it occurred to me that what I had lost was a country. I had never respected the government near to which I lived, but I had foolishly thought that I might manage to live here, minding my private affairs. . . . I dwelt before, perhaps, in the illusion that my life passed somewhere only *between* heaven and hell, but now I cannot persuade myself that I do not dwell wholly within hell."

When John Brown, whom Thoreau had met in 1857, was hanged for his 1859 raid on the federal arsenal at Harper's Ferry, Virginia, many abolitionists in the North conferred martyr status on him. Thoreau was no exception. Brown, he wrote, "could not have been tried by a jury of his peers, because his peers did not exist."

And always, Thoreau continued to walk in the wild places, refreshed by natural beauty—"a genuine product of the soil of New England, a crab apple from the woods, transplanted to a cultivated garden, but retaining the old flavor along with the new," as essayist George Cooke wrote in 1896.

In a poem, *Still River*, Thoreau described a winter walk from Ayer to Lancaster.

> Ploughed and unploughed the fields look all the same,
> White as the youth's first love or ancient's fame;
> Alone the chopper's axe awakes the hills,
> And echoing snap the ice-encumbered rills.

"He was one of those who keep so much of the boy in them that he could never pass a berry without picking it," Channing wrote, describing his friend as a "mystic."

In 1860, Thoreau caught a cold while counting tree rings in Walden Woods. His tuberculosis returned and, while the

Civil War raged, he died on May 6, 1862. His only surviving sibling Sophia, with help from Emerson and Channing, published much of his work posthumously. Thoreau's influence continued to increase in the century and a half after his death. Hawthorne and Louisa May Alcott were among those who heard Emerson's eerily omniscient eulogy at the funeral.

"I have repeatedly known young men of sensibility converted in a moment to the belief that this man was the man they were in search of, the man of men, who could tell them all they should do," Emerson said. "It was a pleasure and a privilege to walk with him. . . . The country knows not yet, or in the least part, how great a son it has lost."

16

Lucy Stone, 1818–1893
"A soul as free as the air"

As Lucy Stone lay dying from stomach cancer in her home overlooking Boston Harbor, her doctor told her to be serene. "There is nothing," she replied, "to be unserene about."

She was gladdened by the news that women's suffrage—the cause she had given her life to—had become law in New Zealand. In her final days, Stone revisited in her mind Coy's Hill, the farm she had grown up on in West Brookfield—the musical brooks, the fields, the singing birds, the autumn leaves, and the lamb that jumped rope with her. She told her husband and daughter that she had much to be thankful for, that life on earth was beautiful and she fully expected the next life to be even better.

In the late afternoon of October 18, 1893, she called her daughter to her side.

"She was very weak," Alice Stone Blackwell later wrote. "She seemed to wish to say something. I put my ear to her lips. She said distinctly, 'Make the world better!'"

Lucy Stone had done her part in making the world better. She was a small woman, but fearless. She was a righteous woman, but kind and good-natured. Andrea Moore Kerr, author of *Lucy Stone: Speaking Out for Equality*, wrote in 1992, "Stone posed a challenge to credibility: she was a noble woman, selfless to a fault; she hewed to the high ground, leaving her

Lucy Stone

biographer to grasp at flaws." One of Stone's contemporaries observed that in her later years, Lucy looked like "the grandmother of all good children."

Stone was the first woman to speak full-time for women's rights, the first woman from the state of Massachusetts to earn a college degree, and the first woman to keep her birth name after marriage. She even proved to be a groundbreaker after her death—she became the first person to be cremated in the Commonwealth. Blazing a path came naturally to her—as a young woman she had traveled alone around the United States in burning hot sun and freezing cold, spreading her message of equal rights for all. She had eggs, books, and insults thrown at her. Her soothing voice and disarming ways won many converts, but her life was not an easy one.

"It was so hard and so difficult that if I had been put at the foot of the loftiest peak of the Rocky Mountains with a jackknife in hand, and had been told, 'Hew your way up,' it would have been pasttime [sic] compared to my task," Stone wrote.

By her request, six men and six women served as her pallbearers. Thousands attended Stone's funeral. The *Boston Globe*'s front page included the headline, "Lucy Stone is dead." The *New York Times* carried a ten-paragraph obituary. Editorial writers around the country predicted she would some day be honored with a statue in Washington, D.C. That never happened, though, and even today her seminal role in suffrage is often underplayed because of a twenty-one-year falling out with Susan B. Anthony and Elizabeth Cady Stanton. During those two decades, Anthony and Stanton wrote the book on women's rights, literally, and intentionally minimized Stone's contribution in their *History of Woman Suffrage*. Although reconciliation would later take place—Anthony would publicly state she had been drawn to suffrage by Lucy Stone—the damage had been done in permanent ink.

Perhaps that slight was in some way fitting. In her eulogy of Abby Kelley Foster, a fellow abolitionist and women's rights advocate, Stone quoted an 1851 speech in which Kelley Foster said, "Sisters, bloody feet wore smooth the path by which you come up here." Stone too paid a heavy price for her devotion. Her only daughter, who also became a leader in the women's rights movement, wrote years later that her mother had subtly guided her toward a more rounded life than her own.

But what a singular life it was for Lucy Stone. It began on August 13, 1818, as the eighth of nine children in a farm family. Stone's grandfather, Francis Stone, had fought in the Revolution and was a leader in Shays' Rebellion. Lucy's father, also named Francis, a hard worker and hard drinker, had previously operated a tannery in Brookfield. Even after he sold the tannery and the family moved to a clapboard farmhouse on Coy's Hill in West Brookfield, his drinking buddies would show up and Francis would insist that his overworked wife Hannah cook for them. Two of Hannah Matthew Stone's children had died in infancy and three more would predecease her. Her children would recall their deeply religious mother's life as one of endless toil.

Hannah had milked eight cows on the night of August 12 and felt labor pains early the next morning while the males in the family were out in the fields trying to save the hay from a drenching rain. When told of the sex of the baby, Hannah said, "Oh, dear! I am sorry it is a girl. A woman's life is so hard!"

In the early nineteenth century, a woman had fewer rights in a family than a minor child. A man owned all of the family's property and even in his death, it went to his children, not to his wife. Wife-beating, using the English "rule of thumb" [the stick used could be no thicker than a man's thumb], was sanctioned in some states, although not in Massachusetts. No college or university admitted women. No public high schools for girls existed, and few occupations were opened to females. Moody and often drunk on cider, Francis Stone beat his children, including Lucy, although she would later insist her childhood was mostly happy. Her greatest joy was running around with her siblings and their dog on the hilly farm overlooking central-western Massachusetts.

"What an opulent home it was," she would later write. "Barrels of meat, and my father used to drive to the Connecticut River and bring home a great wagon-load of shad, and have it salted down, and we ate it all through the year, freshened and cooked with cream; and such abundance of apples . . . .We all worked hard, but we all worked in together, and had the feeling that everything was ours."

Stone clearly loved her mother and much of her life's work was motivated by Hannah's plight. But she did not hate her father. "I will not have my father blamed," she later told her own daughter. "It is enough simply to say that he had the Puritan idea that women were to be governed, and that he had the right to hold the purse, and to rule his own house."

At sixteen, the diminutive Lucy had country girl good looks—rosy cheeks, clear eyes, and long silky brown hair. Despite overtures from several young men, she had already decided she would never marry. That year, she took a teaching job in New Braintree, and in January 1837, another in Paxton. She resented being paid less than male teachers and the wheels of reform had already started turning in her mind. Her brother Bowman, who was studying to be a preacher, subscribed to William Lloyd Garrison's the *Liberator*. In that newspaper, Lucy saw an engraving depicting a female slave in chains over the caption "Am I Not A Woman and A Sister?" and in an editorial Garrison urged female readers to look at the picture and "weep, and speak, and act in their behalf." Lucy also began to read the writing of female abolitionists, including Sarah and Angelina Grimké, daughters of a South Carolina plantation owner, who had freed their slaves and come north to speak for the antislavery movement. Abby Kelley, a Worcester schoolteacher, soon joined the sisters at the podium. Stone would later write in admiration, "Public speaking by women was regarded as something monstrous but they held fast. . . . Literally taking their lives in their hands, they went out to speak."

At an 1837 conference in North Brookfield, an association of Massachusetts ministers issued the "Brookfield Bull," warning churches against the use of their pulpit by antislavery speakers, especially by female speakers, whom they considered "unnatural." Lucy was furious when she heard the Bull read in her church. In 1838, a young Brookfield clergyman defied the ban and invited Abby Kelley to speak from his pulpit. The Stone family was among the crowd that packed the church that evening. Lucy recalled the excitement of the women leaving the church, of dogs barking and her father saying, "When the sluts are out, the dogs will bark."

In August 1843, at twenty-five years old and over her father's objections, Stone went to Oberlin in Ohio, the only co-ed, multi-racial college in the country. In her junior year, Lucy and Antoinette Brown, who would become Stone's lifelong best friend and who was studying to be a preacher, began a women's debating society. On August 1, 1846, Stone gave her first public address at a local antislavery meeting. The *Cleveland Leader* reporter wrote that her speech "gave evidence that a mind naturally brilliant had not been dimmed, but polished rather, by classical studies and the higher mathematics."

From then on, Stone spent much of her time at Oberlin debating classmates, and invariably, "that little blue-eyed girl in the calico gown from Massachusetts" got the best of her male and female opponents. She succeeded in bringing Abby Kelley and her new husband Stephen Foster to Oberlin to speak. As class valedictorian, she won the right to write the graduation address but refused when told she couldn't deliver it herself. Garrison and Frederick Douglass went to Oberlin for an antislavery rally the week she graduated and Garrison met Stone for the first time. To his wife, he wrote, "Lucy Stone . . . has a soul as free as the air and is preparing to go forth as a lecturer, particularly in vindication of the rights of woman."

During her senior year, Stone had informed Kelley and her parents that she intended to become a professional speaker on women's rights. Her brother Frank supported her decision: "If you think you have got brass enough, and can do more good by giving public lectures than any other way, I say go to it" he wrote to her. "But Mother doesn't like the idea."

Lucy would not be dissuaded. After graduating from Oberlin as the first Massachusetts woman to be awarded a college degree, she agreed to become a speaker with the Antislavery Society. She told her mother, "I surely would not be a public speaker if I sought a life of ease, for it will be a most laborious one; nor would I do it for the sake of honor, for I know that I shall be disesteemed, nay, even hated, by some who are now my friends, or who profess to be . . . I expect to plead not for the slave only, but for suffering humanity everywhere. Especially do I mean to labor for the elevation of my sex."

Even in the North, antislavery speakers were often harassed by angry mobs. Female lecturers were particularly vilified, believed to be associated with atheism and free love. Stone's parents remained adamant that she would disgrace the family by speaking publicly, even after her first successful speech on women's rights in her brother's church in Gardner. With each successive engagement, Stone polished her voice—invariably described as "beautiful" or "angelic"—learning how to modulate her tone and how to project into the farthest corners of New England churches, town halls, and packed auditoriums.

"Crowds gathered to heckle and stayed to cheer," Kerr wrote. "After hearing her talk, one reporter gushed, 'I have never, anywhere, heard a speaker whose style of eloquence I more admired: the pride of her acquaintances, the idol of the crowd, wherever she goes, the people en masse turn out to hear Lucy Stone.'"

Stone spoke without notes and eschewed the flowery language of many orators. She used plain words and poignant stories while speaking for the Antislavery Society. She was chided by one organizer for incorporating women's rights into her presentation so she responded, "I was a woman before I was an abolitionist," and offered to resign. Instead, they struck a deal to split her speeches—women's rights on weekdays without pay, abolition on weekends for pay.

In 1848, Lucretia Mott and Elizabeth Cady Stanton headed up a small women's rights gathering in Seneca Falls, New York. The one hundred women at the conference, the first of its kind in the nation, adopted Stanton's "Declaration of Rights and Sentiments" which proposed legal equality and the right to vote for women. Stone did not attend, but continued to speak on her own for women's rights. At first she passed the hat, but soon realized that charging admission brought in more money and also kept more "hoodlums" from attending and harassing her. Still, she had eggs thrown at her, a fire hose trained on her through an open window, and a hymnbook hurled at her head with such force that it knocked her down. Undaunted, she soon began wearing bloomers (knee-length undergarments under a shorter skirt), further consternating her detractors.

In 1850, despite a recent bout of typhoid fever, Stone attended the first national convention on women's rights in Worcester. More than one thousand men and women crowded into Brinley Hall and many more were turned away. The list of speakers included Lucretia Mott, Stephen and Abby Kelley Foster, Sojourner Truth, Frederick Douglass, William Lloyd Garrison, Antoinette Brown—and Lucy Stone.

"We want to be something more than the appendages of society; we want that woman should be the coequal and help-meet of man in all the interest and perils and enjoyments of human life," Stone said when it was her turn to speak. "We want that when she dies, it may not be written on her grave-stone that she was the 'relict' of somebody."

The crowd went wild. Susan B. Anthony would later say a press report of Stone's speech is what drew her into the women's rights movement. The *New York Herald* ridiculed the attendees as "that motley gathering of fanatical radicals, of old grannies, male and female, of fugitive slaves and fugitive lunatics," but Horace Greeley's *New York Tribune* extensively and favorably covered the convention. In the autumn of 1851, Stone organized the second national convention in Worcester and then left to lecture in New England, the Midwest, and Canada, where she outdrew Jenny Lind, the most famous singer of the day.

In 1853, Stone addressed the Massachusetts Legislature. Henry Brown Blackwell, the son of reformers from Cincinnati and the brother of two of the nation's first female physicians, sat in the audience. Henry, or Harry as he was often called, was immediately smitten and decided against all odds to persuade Lucy Stone to marry him. After two years, she finally said yes and they—despite occasional discord caused mostly by his hare-brained business schemes—became partners in her life's work. At their wedding in April 1855, they read a protest "against the present laws of marriage [which] refuse to recognize the wife as an independent, rational being." Stone also caused a controversy, even among her fellow suffragists, by keeping her own name. Her best friend, the Reverend Antoinette Brown by then as she had been ordained the nation's first female minister, married Blackwell's brother the next year.

Stone kept lecturing until Alice was born in 1857. For the next few years, she limited her public appearances, refusing to be away from her daughter overnight. Stone also gave birth in 1859 to a premature son who died almost immediately. Reverend Brown also had a baby in 1857 and Elizabeth Stanton was nursing her sixth child.

"Those of you who have talent to do honor to poor—oh! how poor—womanhood have all given yourselves over to baby-making; and left poor brainless me to do battle alone," Susan B. Anthony wrote.

When the Civil War started in 1861, all reforms were put on hold. After the war, Stone championed political rights and suffrage for black slaves as well as for women. When the states ratified the Fourteenth Amendment in 1868 and the Fifteenth Amendment in 1870, however, black men—but not white or black women—had won the right to vote.

That set up a schism that divided Stone from Stanton and Anthony for two decades. Stone, although deeply disappointed that women were not included, still supported the amendments. "We are lost if we turn from the middle principle and argue for one class," she said. Anthony and Stanton did not agree, and fell in league with an unstable, self-declared presidential candidate named George Francis Train. The wealthy Train agreed to finance a woman's newspaper, the *Revolution*, but on the condition it would include his anti-black and anti-Republican editorials. Most suffragists were Republicans, the party of Lincoln.

"Stanton agreed with Train," Elisabeth Griffith wrote in *In Her Own Right: The Life of Elizabeth Cady Stanton* in 1984. "She also wanted to exclude blacks and immigrants from citizenship unless women were enfranchised at the same time. She did not like being put in an inferior legal position when she considered herself a superior person. . . . She elevated superior womanhood and derided 'Sambo.'"

The schism between Stanton and Anthony's group in New York and Stone's suffragettes in New England—Stanton called them the "Boston malcontents" in a signed *Revolution* editorial—led to the forming of two organizations, the National Woman Suffrage Association and the American Woman Suffrage Association. Things got even worse when Stanton's Nationals took up with Victoria C. Woodhull, an advocate of free love who was often quoted as saying, "A woman has a right to take a new lover every day if she chooses."

That was a serious problem for suffragists like Stone because they had always battled suspicions that free love and the destruction of marriage were their goals. Stanton's refusal to admit men to the national association, her race-based opposition to the Fifteenth Amendment, her association with Woodhull, and her own call for easy divorce shocked her former allies in Boston. To many reformers, Stanton became an embarrassment. After the split in 1869, Stone, Henry Blackwell, and others in the American branch started their own newspaper, the *Woman's Journal*. The *Journal* outlived the *Revolution* and became the "voice" of the suffrage movement after the two sides finally reunited in 1890.

In her later years, Lucy Stone edited the *Journal* in her office in Boston's South Station and cared for the animals and the vegetable garden at the family's home in Dorchester, high on a bluff overlooking the harbor and Neponset River.

"She once said, 'There was a good farmer spoiled when I went into reform,'" Alice Stone Blackwell wrote in her 1930 biography of her mother, *Lucy Stone, Pioneer of Woman's Rights*. "There was always a certain country strength and simplicity about her. She was an admirable housekeeper, of the old New England type. She dried all the herbs and put up all the fruits in their season. She made her own yeast, her own bread, her own dried beef, even her own soap. . . . She was the most motherly of women. She was attracted by all children, dirty or clean, pretty or ugly."

Even as her health failed, Stone continued to work for suffrage. In her last speech at the Chicago World's Fair in the summer of 1893, she talked about the progress of the past fifty years. "We endeavored to create that wholesome discontent in women that would compel them to reach out after far better things," she said. "But every new step was a trial and a conflict."

Within months, her stomach cancer wore her down to the point where all she could do is sit on her patio on pleasant autumn afternoons with a favorite black cat in her lap.

"She was perfectly calm and fearless, and made all her preparations to go as quietly as if she were only going into the next room," Alice wrote. "She said, 'I know the Eternal Order, and I believe in it. I have not a fear, or a dread, or a doubt.'"

After Lucy died, Henry said to his daughter as they walked from her deathbed, "We must try to keep Mamma's flag flying."

They did, both working tirelessly for suffrage. Henry edited the *Woman's Journal* until he died sixteen years later. Many nights, Alice wrote, he sat alone in the dark in Lucy's room hoping her spirit would come to him. Of the many tributes that poured in after Stone's death, the greatest may have come from her old nemesis. "The death of no woman in America had ever called out so general a tribute of public respect and esteem," Elizabeth Cady Stanton wrote.

Lucy Stone's best friend, sister-in-law, and fellow suffragist, the Reverend Antoinette Brown, preached her last sermon in 1916. On November 2, 1920, at ninety-five years old, in poor health and almost blind, she exercised her newly won right to vote.

17

Helen Hunt Jackson, 1830–1885
A Woman with a Cause

Helen Hunt buried her husband and both of her children before she turned thirty-five. Her husband, U.S. Army major Edward Hunt, died in 1863 while testing a one-man submarine. Their son, nine-year-old Rennie, died from diphtheria a year and a half later. Their only other child, Murray, had died from scarlet fever in 1854 while an infant.

The suddenly childless widow—lifelong friend of fellow Amherst native and classmate Emily Dickinson—turned to writing poetry to assuage her grief, and to journalism and fiction to make a living. Within a decade, Ralph Waldo Emerson pronounced her "the greatest woman poet" and said her work was better than that of most of the well-known male poets.

Hunt moved to the drier climate of Colorado in 1873 on a doctor's advice—she suffered from recurring bronchitis—and met a wealthy railroad magnate named William Sharpless Jackson there. They married in 1875. Freed from financial concerns, Helen Hunt Jackson was able to concentrate on her writing and her fascination with the American West.

On a trip back home to Massachusetts in 1879, she met Standing Bear, and that meeting determined the rest of her life.

"I have done now, I believe, the last of the things I have said I would never do," she wrote to a friend. "I have become

Helen Hunt Jackson

what I have said a thousand times was the most odious thing in the world—a woman with a cause."

And what a cause it was. Standing Bear was a chief of the Ponca and his tribe's tale is one of the saddest stories in our nation's treatment of Native Americans. For centuries, the peaceful Ponca lived between the Missouri and Niobrara rivers in Nebraska near the South Dakota border. The Ponca lived in permanent villages, grew corn, and went on a yearly buffalo hunt. Many became Christians. The Ponca had signed peace treaties with the United States government in 1858, 1859, and 1865 that guaranteed them their traditional lands.

"The Ponca bothered no white man," Stephen Dando-Collins wrote in his 2004 book, *Standing Bear is a Person*. "Fewer than a thousand men, women and children in all, they lived in peace and solitude on their little reservation, having nothing to do with the skirmishes that the larger Sioux, Cheyenne, Comanche, and Arapaho tribes were having with the U.S. Army in the 1860s."

In 1868, though, in what would be a failed attempt to appease the Sioux, the federal government mistakenly included the Ponca's land in the Great Sioux Reservation. Emboldened by the government's mistake, Brule Sioux raiding parties began attacking the Ponca.

Things got worse for the Ponca after gold was discovered in the Black Hills and the federal government proceeded to break every treaty it had with the Sioux and Cheyenne who lived there. In 1876, the government sent the army to South Dakota to protect prospectors. On June 25, the over-confident Lt. Colonel George Armstrong Custer and 266 of his men in the Seventh Calvary were killed within minutes after they stumbled upon Crazy Horse and 5,000 warriors camped at the Little Big Horn.

"Custer's Massacre" caused hysteria in the East and petrified politicians in Washington, who quickly passed legislation authorizing the forced removal of aggressive northern tribes to Indian Territory in what is now Oklahoma. The Ponca, who had not participated in the Battle of the Little Big Horn, and who, in fact, had never been involved in any fighting with whites, were erroneously included on the list of tribes to be removed.

In February 1877, an Indian Affairs agent brought Standing Bear and nine other elderly Ponca chiefs south and told them to pick out a reservation in the barren Indian Territory. The old chiefs refused—they loved their own fertile land and could see what living in Oklahoma had done to the ill and indolent Cherokee, Choctaw, and Seminoles—tribes who had been forcibly removed from the Southeast decades earlier. The agent became so angry with the uncooperative Ponca that he left the elderly chiefs there, forcing them to walk six hundred miles home in the winter. Surviving on handouts and corn-husks, sleeping huddled together in snowdrifts and abandoned barns, the old men somehow made their way back to Nebraska two months later.

Shortly after they arrived home, though, the U.S. Army forced the entire Ponca tribe, all 752 members, to leave their log homes, barns, and plows behind and to march to Oklahoma at bayonet point. As soon as they were out of sight, the army tore down the Ponca's houses and their sawmill and gristmill, and Indian Affairs confiscated, and apparently sold off, their tools, livestock, and all of their possessions. Standing Bear's daughter Prairie Flower and many other Ponca died on the long journey south and many more died from disease in Oklahoma—158 in the first year alone. Six hundred of their seven hundred ponies also died in that first year. The Ponca protested their treatment as well as they could. Standing Bear even won an audience with President Rutherford B. Hayes in Washington, but the president did nothing to help the heartbroken Ponca return to their rightful lands.

As the winter of 1878–1879 began, many Ponca sickened. In December, as he lay dying in Indian Territory, Standing Bear's teenage son Bear Shield whispered a wish to his sobbing father—he wanted to be buried with his ancestors on the

Niobrara so he would not be doomed to wander the afterlife alone. On January 2, 1879, Standing Bear and twenty-six other Ponca—including Standing Bear's infant grandson and grand-daughter whom he and his wife adopted after Prairie Flower died—slipped out of Oklahoma with the body of Bear Shield in a wagon. They headed north again.

When they arrived in Nebraska at the end of February, famed Indian fighter General George Crook arrested and jailed them at Fort Omaha. But Crook was so moved by the Ponca's plight that he tipped off *Omaha Daily Herald* editor Thomas Henry Tibbles to the tragic story unfolding. Tibbles, with the aid of Susette "Bright Eyes" La Flesche as his inter-preter, interviewed Standing Bear and other Poncas. The 5-foot-tall Bright Eyes was the daughter of Iron Eyes, chief of the Omaha, a tribe closely related to the Ponca. Tibbles also convinced two Nebraska lawyers to represent Standing Bear pro bono. The ensuing trial—based on the lawyers' argument that Standing Bear was a man under the Fourteenth Amend-ment and had a citizen's rights—attracted national attention.

With Bright Eyes translating, Standing Bear held up his hand as he testified at the trial.

"This hand is not the color of yours but if I pierce it I shall feel pain," he said. "The blood that flows from it will be the same color as yours. I am a man. The same God made us both."

Standing Bear's eloquence moved U.S. District Court Judge Elmer Dundy, General Crook, and everyone else in the courtroom to tears. Dundy then ruled—sixteen years after Lin-coln's Emancipation Proclamation—"an Indian is a person. . . . [and has] the inalienable right to life, liberty, and the pursuit of happiness."

After the trial, Standing Bear, along with Tibbles, Tib-bles's new bride Bright Eyes, and Bright Eyes's brother Frank La Flesche, went East on a speaking tour to tell the Ponca's story, to raise money for the now destitute and homeless tribe, and to raise America's awareness of the injustices being perpetrated on America's native people. Helen Hunt Jackson, then forty-nine and on a visit back East to attend Oliver Wendell Holmes's birthday party, covered a speech by Standing Bear in Boston on November 1 as a correspondent for the *New York Independent*. She wrote under the byline H.H.

"Within days, Jackson had approached Henry Tibbles about joining the crusaders on tour," Dando-Collins wrote. "Jackson became the fifth member of the team, a mentor for Bright Eyes and a motivator for them all. Both Standing Bear and Bright Eyes became extremely fond of H.H. She would have been present later that month when Bright Eyes became the first woman ever to speak at Boston's famous Faneuil Hall and Standing Bear the first Native American to do so."

Jackson threw herself into the cause of Indian rights— "I shall be found with 'Indians' engraved on my brain when I am dead," she wrote in December 1879. "A fire has been kindled in me which will never go out." Before she died five and a half years later, Helen Hunt Jackson had published a groundbreaking study about the government's treatment of Native Americans, *A Century of Dishonor*, and a celebrated novel, *Ramona*, that she hoped would do for Native Americans what her friend Harriet Beecher Stowe's *Uncle Tom's Cabin* had done for blacks.

Hunt Jackson was born Helen Marie Fiske on October 14, 1830, daughter of Nathan and Deborah Fiske. Her father taught Greek and Latin at Amherst College and had previously been a Congregational minister. Helen's mother, Deborah Vinal Fiske, a writer of children's stories, found Helen much wilder than her sister Ann.

"Helen learns very well, but I do not drive her very much to make her very literary," her mother wrote to a cousin. "She is quite inclined to question the author of everything; the Bible she says does not feel as if it were true."

When Helen was thirteen, Deborah Fiske sickened with tuberculosis, and Helen was sent to two boarding schools, the Ipswich Female Seminary in Massachusetts and the Abbott

Institute in New York City. Her mother died when she was sixteen and her father died three years later.

In 1852, Helen Fiske, always described as "vivacious," married U.S. Army captain Edward Bissell Hunt, the brother of a former New York governor. For the next eleven years, they moved around the eastern United States as a military family, including four stops in Newport, Rhode Island, where she socialized with writer Henry Wadsworth Longfellow and reformer Lydia Maria Child. Tragedy stalked the marriage however. Murray, the Hunts' first child, died in 1854 when he was less than one year old. In 1863, Major Hunt suffocated while experimenting with his one-man submarine he was working on as a weapon to be used in the Civil War. Less than two years later, nine-year-old Rennie died from diphtheria.

Alone at thirty-five, Hunt returned to Newport. With Thomas Wentworth Higginson as her literary mentor, she began writing poetry to alleviate her grief and essays and fiction to support herself. She proved to be a prolific writer, publishing thirty books and hundreds of essays over the next twenty years, and she was immediately successful. "I never write for money. I write for love, then after it is written, I print for money," she wrote to a friend. Her chronic bronchitis, however, forced her to leave New England in 1873 for the drier climate of Colorado. In 1875, she married wealthy William Sharpless Jackson of Colorado Springs. She made another mark in American literary history the next year by sending a letter to her childhood friend back in Amherst. By then, Emily Dickinson had become increasingly reclusive.

"You are a great poet—and it is a wrong to the day you live in, that you will not sing aloud," Jackson wrote. She eventually convinced Dickinson to contribute her "Success is Counted Sweetest" to *A Masque of Poets,* which published it without naming the author in 1878—the only poem by Dickinson published in her lifetime. Jackson also had several poems in that publication.

As was the custom of the time, especially for female writers, Jackson herself published almost all of her work under pseudonyms, most often "H.H." for her nonfiction and "Saxe Holm" for her novels. Her work, including many travel pieces, appeared in the *New York Evening Post*, *Nation*, the *New York Independent*, *Atlantic Monthly*, the *Christian Union*, and various children's magazines. The only efforts she published under her own name were her last and most important books, *A Century of Dishonor* and *Ramona*, writing both after her life-changing meeting with Standing Bear in 1879.

"In a whirlwind of activity, she became a veritable one-person reform movement, circulating petitions and tracts, rebuking editors, army officers, clergymen, college presidents, and congressmen, and filling the press with stinging letters," Francis Paul Prucha wrote in his 1984 book, *The Great Father: The United States Government and the American Indians*.

Popular with the reformers and literary types in the East who formed the Boston Indian Citizenship Committee, the Native American rights cause was abhorred in the West, where many white settlers still feared Indian attacks. Helen Hunt Jackson's defense of the Ute, who were still involved in scattered incidents in Colorado in the early 1880s, and her condemnation in *A Century of Dishonor* of the Sand Creek Massacre of 1864, in which the Colorado First Cavalry had slaughtered and mutilated 150 unarmed Cheyenne and Arapaho—a massacre which had been celebrated with jubilation in Denver—left her "without a sympathizer in the state," according to the Colorado Woman's Hall of Fame.

"It is a trite saying that history repeats itself; but it is impossible to read now these accounts of the massacres of defenseless and peaceable Indians in the middle of the eighteenth century, without the reflection that the record of the nineteenth is blackened by the same stains," Jackson wrote. "What Pennsylvania pioneers did in 1763 to helpless and peaceable Indians of Conestoga, Colorado pioneers did in 1864 to helpless and peaceable Cheyennes at Sand Creek, and have threatened to do again to helpless and peaceable Utes in 1880. The word 'extermination' is as ready on the frontiersman's tongue today as it was a hundred years ago; and the threat is more portentous now, seeing that we are, by a whole century of prosperity, stronger and more numerous, and the Indians are, by a whole century of suffering and oppression, fewer and weaker. But our crime is baser and our infamy deeper in the same proportion."

Jackson had dashed out *A Century of Dishonor* after several months of intense research in the Astor Library in New York City in early 1880. When the book was published in January 1881, she mailed a copy to every member of Congress at her own expense. On the blood red jacket she emblazoned a quote from Benjamin Franklin: "Look at your hands! They are stained with the blood of your relations."

"*A Century of Dishonor* was a strange book, a disorganized, cluttered compilation of fragments, which told the story of the government's relations with seven tribes," Prucha wrote. "It was a polemic, not balanced history, and everywhere evidenced the haste with which it had been put together. . . . The intention was to awaken the conscience of America to the flagrant wrongs that had been perpetrated upon the Indians. . . . Once the people were aroused, she was convinced that they would demand that Congress right the wrongs."

A Century of Dishonor caused a sensation but had little lasting effect. President Chester Arthur appointed Jackson special commissioner of Indian Affairs in 1882, and the next year she returned to southern California—she had previously gone there to write a travel series—to report on the condition of the Mission Indians. A Mission Indian bill, based on her report, failed to pass Congress. (The only comprehensive legislation that sprang from Jackson's advocacy, the well-meaning Dawes Severalty Act, actually backfired. Sponsored by U.S. Senator Henry Dawes of Massachusetts, the aim of the act was to absorb Native Americans into the larger society by dividing up communal tribal lands and allotting individual Indians 160 acres each. The bill was debated for years and finally enacted in 1887.

Within decades, thanks to corruption and swindles, the vast majority of the tribal land in the West was in white hands.)

Frustrated with her effort to affect change, Jackson decided in late 1883 that she would attack the problem through fiction. In December, she began feverishly working on *Ramona,* a historical romance. "In my *Century of Dishonor* I tried to attack people's consciences directly, and they would not listen," she told Higginson. "Now I have sugared my pill, and it remains to be seen if it will go down." She worked obsessively on the novel, which spotlighted the mistreatment of Native Americans and Mexican Americans.

"She wrote . . . with great passion and zeal, succumbing twice to 'nervous prostration' and plagued by a persistent cold," Kelli Olson wrote in *Nineteenth-Century American Women Writers.* "She found herself writing 2,000 to 3,000 words a morning and working late into the night. She drew upon her trips to California for plot, scenery, and characters. In a letter to a friend, she wrote: 'If I can do one-hundredth part for the Indians as Mrs. Stowe did for the Negroes, I will be thankful.'"

Ramona, published in late 1883, was a huge success but not for the reasons Jackson hoped. The romance and Hunt's description of picturesque old California attracted readers more than her message. *Ramona* has gone through three hundred printings and has been made into a stage play and three movies.

In June 1884, Jackson severely fractured her left leg in a fall. Shortly after that, she was diagnosed with cancer. Before she died on August 12, 1885, she sent a letter to President Grover Cleveland urging him to read *A Century of Dishonor.*

"I am dying happier in the belief I have that it is your hand that is destined to strike the first steady blow toward lifting the burden of infamy from our country and righting the wrongs of the Indian race," she wrote. Upon learning of her friend's death, Emily Dickinson wrote a letter to William Sharpless Jackson.

"Helen of Troy will die, but Helen of Colorado, never," the belle of Amherst wrote. "'Dear friend, can you walk?' were the last words that I wrote her. 'Dear friend, I can fly'—her immortal (soaring) reply."

Five years after Hunt's death, three hundred Sioux men, women, and children were killed in the Wounded Knee Massacre, effectively ending the United States government's war on the Plains Indians. Twenty-five soldiers also died. "There is nothing to conceal or apologize for in the Wounded Knee Battle," General E. D. Scott concluded in his report to Congress. "That women and children were casualties was unfortunate but unavoidable. . . . The Indians at Wounded Knee brought their own destruction as surely as any people ever did."

18

Robert Gould Shaw, 1837–1863
"Take the fort or die there"

On June 5, 1890, Henry L. Higginson donated thirty-one acres in Cambridge to Harvard University for athletic playing fields.

"The only other wish on my part," the fifty-six-year-old founder of the Boston Symphony Orchestra wrote, "is that the ground shall be called 'The Soldier's Field,' and marked with a stone bearing the names of some dear friends,—alumni of the University, and noble gentlemen—who gave freely and eagerly all that they had or hoped for, to their country and to their fellow men in the hour of great need—the war of 1861 to 1865 in defense of the Republic: James Savage, Jr., Charles Russell Lowell, Edward Barry Dalton, Stephen George Perkins, James Jackson Lowell, Robert Gould Shaw."

In a speech to Harvard students five days later, Higginson talked about youth, education, and sportsmanship. And he talked about war. He had served in the Union Army with all of the men Soldier's Field was dedicated to—wealthy young Boston Brahmins like himself who answered the call to duty. Unlike any of them, though, he had survived. They had died in the cause of freedom, he said, at places with names like Cedar Mountain and Gettysburg and Fort Wagner.

Higginson told the Harvard men that day about "a sunny-haired, blue-eyed boy."

Robert Gould Shaw
COURTESY OF THE MASSACHUSETTS HISTORICAL SOCIETY

"You should have seen Robert Shaw as he, with his chosen officers, led away from Boston his black men of the 54th Massachusetts amid the cheers of his townsmen," Higginson said.

Twenty-seven years earlier, on July 18, 1863, Shaw had been shot through the heart as he stood on the parapet of Fort Wagner in South Carolina, the 5-foot-5 colonel waving his sword and exhorting his men, "Forward, 54th." Shaw fell forward into the fort, mortally wounded, but his troops pressed on. The Massachusetts 54th, the nation's first regiment of free black men, suffered staggering casualties in hand-to-hand combat that evening—of the 600 who charged the fort, 272 were killed, wounded, or captured—and the Confederates successfully repulsed their assault. The fort was not taken until September 6 after a long siege, yet the charge of the 54th on July 18 proved a turning point in the war. Less than two weeks after the assault, United States senator Charles Sumner of Massachusetts, a friend of Shaw's parents, predicted the death of their twenty-six-year-old son would be, "sacred in history and art."

How right Sumner was. More than forty poets—from Ralph Waldo Emerson to Robert Lowell a century later—were moved to verse by Shaw's heroism. "So nigh is grandeur to our dust, So near is God to man," Emerson wrote. "When Duty whispers low, 'Thou must,' The youth replies, 'I can.'"

Shaw's privileged upbringing, his ultimate conquering of his own prejudices, his embrace of black soldiers as equals, and his glorious death became legend. The 54th's courage and sacrifice spurred black enlistment in the North, ultimately proving the difference in the war. William Harvey Carney, an ex-slave, who saved the 54th's flag, though wounded twice in the battle, later said, "Boys, I only did my duty; the old flag never touched the ground," and was the first black soldier to receive the Congressional Medal of Honor.

After the battle, the Confederates intended to insult Shaw by tossing him into a common grave with his men. "We buried him in the trench with his niggers," Brigadier General Johnson Hagood replied when Union soldiers sought the return of Shaw's corpse. Shaw's grieving father soon wrote a letter to Union General Quincy Gilmore insisting no further effort be made to recover the body. He said there was "no holier place" for his son than "surrounded by his brave and devoted soldiers."

"Hagood little knew that he was giving the dead soldier the most honorable burial that man could have devised," Henry Cabot Lodge wrote in 1918. "The order to bury him with his 'niggers,' which ran through the North and remained fixed in our history, showed, in a flash of light, the hideous barbarism of a system which made such things and such feelings possible."

In death, Shaw has become, "more monument than man," according to Russell Duncan in his 1992 book *Blue-eyed Child of Fortune: The Civil War Letters of Colonel Robert Gould Shaw.* The poorly planned assault was a military disaster—the Union suffered seven times the casualties the Confederates did—but the propaganda value of brave black soldiers led by their beloved white colonel proved bountiful for the Union.

Before the assault on Wagner, many whites in the North remained dubious that blacks would fight for their own liberation—"one Southern regiment of white men would put 20 regiments of them Negroes to flight in an hour," the *Boston Pilot,* newspaper of the rapidly growing Boston Irish community, editorialized. (The Irish Catholic immigrants, who justifiably prided themselves on their fighting ability, had been horribly mistreated themselves in the 1850s in Massachusetts by the abolition-supporting Know Nothing Party, and, as historian Oscar Handlin later wrote, they valued "the security that came from the existence in the country of at least one social class beneath them.")

Black abolitionist Frederick Douglass had been arguing since the war began that free blacks and former slaves should be "formed into a liberating army to march into the South and raise the banner of emancipation" but few in the North, including the president, agreed. "To arm the Negroes would turn 50,000 bayonets from the loyal Border States against us that were for us," Lincoln initially said.

In January 1863, though, after his Emancipation Proclamation had been enacted and desperate for soldiers, Lincoln authorized secretary of war Edwin M. Stanton to enlist black men into volunteer regiments.

"Many people who supported the war for union lashed out at Lincoln for changing the goal of the war to one of freedom of the slaves," Duncan wrote. "The idea of black men in uniforms with guns frightened some Northerners and most Southerners. Many white soldiers loathed the idea of serving with black soldiers."

By late July 1863, the war had become extremely unpopular in the North. The carnage at Gettysburg two weeks earlier had been a particular horror. White volunteers had become scarce. Just days before the assault on Wagner, Irish-born workmen—who feared employment competition from blacks—rioted against the draft in New York City, killing at least eleven black men and burning down a black orphanage.

Although blacks had fought in the Revolution, they had been banned from joining state militias since 1792 and the War Department did not allow them to join the regular army. Blacks did serve in the navy from the start of the Civil War—but only as cooks, stewards, coal heavers, and firefighters.

"The charge upon Wagner changed things," Duncan wrote. "Blacks had proven themselves as fighting men and vindicated their sponsors, the abolitionists. By year's end, sixty black regiments were being organized and they would not be used simply to dig fortifications, handle baggage, and cook food for white soldiers. They would be allowed to fight."

Famed sculptor Augustus Saint-Gaudens spent thirteen years working on a commissioned eleven-foot-by-fourteen-foot bronze relief sculpture that was dedicated on Boston Common in 1897. One reason it took so long is that Saint-Gaudens had to figure out a way to honor Shaw's parents' wish that black soldiers, and not just their son, be included in the piece. In 1989, a movie about the 54th, *Glory*, starring Matthew Broderick as Robert Shaw, won three Oscars, including best supporting actor for Denzel Washington.

What made a young man of privilege, a party boy, turn into a hero? What made Robert Gould Shaw, who initially called his black volunteers "darkeys" in letters to friends, and who privately doubted their courage and ability, so convinced of their bravery and their equality that he begged his commanders to let them fight? Honor is the answer to the first question—"Many young 'aristocrats' like Robert Gould Shaw became officers in black regiments not only because of their devotion to the abolition cause but also because of a sense of class pride and noblesse oblige," Keith P. Wilson wrote in his 2002 book *Campfires of Freedom.*

The recognition of an essential truth—his black soldiers were indeed men—answers the second.

Shaw was born in Boston on October 10, 1837, the only son of Francis and Sarah Shaw. He had four sisters. His grandfather had made a fortune in investments and Shaw's parents, not needing to work for money, worked for social causes, particularly the abolition of slavery. In addition to Sumner, they counted publisher William Lloyd Garrison, Massachusetts governor John A. Andrew, Lydia Child, Wendell Phillips, and Douglass among their abolitionist friends.

When Robert was five, the family moved to West Roxbury next to Brook Farm, a Utopian communal experiment. The Shaws then lived on Staten Island for a time. In 1851 they sailed for Europe. Teenaged Robert Shaw—called Rob by his family and Bob by his friends—spent the next four years attending schools in Switzerland, Italy, and Germany, reading novels and playing violin.

He entered Harvard in 1856 as a member of what would become known as "The Fighting Class of 1860." He played sports, went to parties, joined the debating society, and visited his sister Susie who was also going to school in Cambridge. He dropped out after his junior year to work for his uncle in a mercantile office in New York.

In 1860, the long simmering dispute between the North and South over slavery came to a boil. Compromises over the issue—especially the Compromise of 1850 with its Fugitive Slave law and the Kansas-Nebraska Act in 1854—had only exacerbated the rift. Rhetoric on both sides grew increasingly hotter throughout the 1850s—when Sumner denounced a fellow senator in 1856 for causing pro-slavery violence in Kansas, a South Carolina representative caned Sumner into insensibility.

John Brown's attempt to seize the federal arsenal at Harper's Ferry in 1859 with the hopes of starting a slave insurrection resulted in his hanging, and further divided the country. Many Northerners saw him as a martyr while Southerners saw Brown—and all abolitionists—as dangerous zealots.

Lincoln's election to the presidency in November 1860 made the Civil War inevitable. Although a moderate on slavery compared to the men he beat for the Republican nomination, his platform included no expansion of slavery and he had long held that the United States could not survive as "a house divided." Lincoln won the election—the only one Shaw ever voted in—by beating three candidates put forth by a split Democratic Party.

"The Republican platform . . . embodied the political and economic programs of the North," Bruce Catton wrote in *The American Heritage New History of the Civil War.* "But by now a singular fatalism gripped the nation. . . . Men could talk only about slavery, and on that subject they could neither talk nor, for the most part, even think, with moderation."

A month after the election, South Carolina seceded from the Union. Mississippi, Alabama, Georgia, Florida, Louisiana and Texas quickly followed, and in February, they formed the Confederates States of America. In his inaugural address on March 4, 1861, Lincoln promised to "hold, occupy and possess" all federal property in the South. Catton theorizes that each side still thought the other was bluffing.

"Neither side realized until it was too late that the other side was desperately in earnest," Catton wrote. "The Southern orator who promised to wipe up, with his handkerchief, all of the blood that would be spilled because of secession was expressing a very common viewpoint."

On April 5, Robert Gould Shaw, then twenty-three, wrote to his sister Susie from New York. Like many of his friends, Shaw found the possibility of war exhilarating and had signed up for a thirty-day enlistment with the 7th Regiment of the New York State Militia.

"It is now almost certain that Mr. Lincoln is going to re-enforce the United States forts, and in that case the Southern-ers will almost surely resist," he wrote. "For my part I want to see the Southern States either brought back by force, or else recognized as independent."

On the morning of April 12, rebel soldiers from South Carolina began firing mortars at federally occupied Fort Sumter in Charleston Harbor and the war was on. Lincoln called for 75,000 men to rush to Washington to defend the Capitol. The New York 7th was among the first to respond. They marched through a two-mile "tempest of cheers" in New York City on their way to the ferry.

"You mustn't think, dear Sue, that any of us are going to be killed; for they are collecting such a force there that an attack would be insane," Shaw wrote to his sister.

The 7th saw no action in Washington. When his thirty days ended, Shaw joined the Massachusetts 2nd with many of his Harvard friends and deployed to South Carolina. Despite Virginia, Arkansas, North Carolina, and Tennessee having joined the Confederacy by then, the Massachusetts men were involved in only a few skirmishes before setting up winter quarters in Maryland, where Shaw's father, Susie, and Susie's friend, Annie Haggerty, visited him.

Then the real fighting for the 2nd began. In May 1862, Stonewall Jackson's troops routed the 2nd in the Shenandoah Valley. Shaw was slightly wounded but his gold watch saved his life. "The ball would undoubtedly have entered my stomach, and as it was, bruised my hip a good deal," he wrote home. In August, the 2nd suffered great casualties at Cedar Mountain in a withering crossfire. Of 427 enlisted men, 157 were killed, wounded or missing although "not under fire more than 30 minutes." Of twenty-two officers, five—all close friends of Shaw's—were killed. Five others were wounded and four captured.

Shaw, now a captain, wrote to Higginson, who was recovering from a wound in Boston: "All our officers behaved nobly. . . . It was splendid to see [them] walk straight up into the shower of bullets as if it were so much rain; men who, until this year, had lived lives of perfect ease and luxury. O, it is hard to believe that we shall never see them again."

On September 15, the 2nd Massachusetts fought in the Battle of Antietam—which included the bloodiest single day—23,000 combined casualties—in the history of the United States. After the costly Union victory, Lincoln issued his Emancipation Proclamation freeing all slaves in states remaining in rebellion as of January 1. "For my part, I can't see what practical good it can do now," Shaw wrote home. "Jeff Davis will soon issue a proclamation threatening to hang every prisoner they take, and will make this a war of extermination."

He was right. Davis, the president of the Confederacy, promised to execute any captured black soldiers—or white officers leading black troops.

In the autumn, Shaw proposed to Annie Haggerty by mail, and on his visit to her home in Lenox in December, she accepted.

"I have thought a great deal of you—indeed almost all the time since I left Lenox—and of my visit to you, especially the last part of it," he wrote to her when he returned to his unit.

On February 2, 1863, Governor Andrew offered Shaw the Colonelcy of the 54th Massachusetts Regiment, which would be the first black regiment raised in a free state. At first, Shaw declined, but his mother urged him to accept and he did.

"This is my reward for asking [for] my children not early honors, but souls to see the right and courage to follow it," Sarah Shaw wrote to her son.

Robert Shaw returned to Boston and recruits for the 54th began arriving at Camp Meigs in Readville (present-day Hyde Park). On May 2, he married Annie in New York City. They had a brief honeymoon in Lenox and Shaw returned to his men for three more weeks of training.

By the middle of May, 1,007 black men from 24 states had joined the regiment's 37 white officers. Some of the men had been born free, while others were ex-slaves. More than half of the enlisted men were farmers and laborers, but barbers, seamen, waiters, teamsters, cabinetmakers, and a dentist and druggist also signed on. Two of Frederick Douglass's sons were among the recruits.

At 9:00 a.m. on May 28th, the 54th Massachusetts marched to the statehouse for review on Boston Common. Thousands of well-wishers lined the streets and cheered as the 54th marched by. Shaw's family watched the parade from the second-floor balcony of Sarah Shaw's parents' home at 44 Beacon Street.

"I was not quite eighteen when the regiment sailed," Shaw's sister Ellen later wrote. "My mother, Rob's wife, my sisters and I were on the balcony to see the regiment go by, and when Rob riding at its head, looked up and kissed his sword, his face was as the face of an angel and I felt perfectly sure he would never come back."

After the review, the 54th marched to Battery Wharf and boarded a transport ship for South Carolina. The 54th was assigned to work under Colonel James Montgomery, who led the 2nd South Carolina, a "contraband" unit made up of slaves freed by the army.

To Shaw and his men's disappointment, they were initially assigned noncombat work. In early June, Montgomery's troops plundered Darien, Georgia, and set the buildings on fire even though they had encountered no resistance there. Only one company of the 54th was compelled to take part in the firing, but Shaw was furious about Montgomery's "barbarous sort of warfare" and complained to headquarters. Later in June, Shaw's men learned they would be paid three dollars less per month than white soldiers were paid. Shaw wrote a letter of protest and the men and officers all refused any pay for eighteen months until the government acquiesced.

On July 6, Shaw sent a missive asking headquarters to let his men fight "in order that they may have witnesses beside their own officers to what they are capable of doing."

He soon got his wish. On July 11, General Gilmore's troops had attacked Fort Wagner on the north end of Morris Island but were driven back. Gilmore ordered a steady naval bombardment of the fort and made plans for a second assault.

On July 16, four companies of the 54th Massachusetts were on picket duty on a nearby island with the white soldiers of the 10th Connecticut when Confederates attacked. The 54th held valiantly, losing fourteen dead and eighteen wounded, but allowing the Connecticut men an avenue to escape. One Connecticut soldier wrote the 54th "fought like heroes." That night, Shaw wrote to Annie, "Good bye, darling, for the night. I know this letter will give you pleasure, because what we have done today wipes out the memory of the Darien affair, which you could not but grieve over, though we were innocent participators."

The next day, General George Strong asked Shaw if the 54th would lead the assault on Wagner. Shaw accepted, desperately wanting to prove his men's bravery. About 6:30 p.m. on Saturday July 18, Shaw gave a correspondent for the *New York Daily Tribune* some personal papers and asked him to send them to his family if he was killed. He then rode to where the regiment was formed on the beach and dismounted. He smoked a cigar, visited with his men, and told them they could prove themselves with the nation watching.

"Shaw challenged the men, 'take the fort or die there'" Duncan wrote, "They promised to try."

At 7:45 p.m., the 54th moved forward through heavy sand and, at times, water up to their knees.

Nearing the fort, Shaw ordered quick-time, then double-quick. When they reached one hundred yards from Wagner, a fierce Rebel volley stunned the first battalion. Shaw yelled, "Forward 54th" and his men charged through a ditch and gained the parapet on the right. Shaw was one of the first to scale the sandy wall. He stood for a second on top, and, urging his men on, was shot through the heart and fell forward into the fort. His men continued to fight in savage hand-to-hand combat for an hour before being driven back. Subsequent assaults by white regiments also failed. The next morning, the Rebels rejected a federal request to recover the Union dead and began burying the more than eight hundred bodies lying in the sand.

The Rebels divided up Shaw's uniform and personal belongings. They threw his corpse into the bottom of a pit and piled the bodies of twenty black enlisted men on top of him.

Two days after the assault on Fort Wagner, Colonel Charles Lowell, who had married Shaw's sister Josephine, wrote home.

"Everything that comes about Rob shows his death to have been more and more completely that, which every soldier, and every man, must long to die. But it is given to very few, for very few do their duty as Rob did. I am thankful that they buried him with his [soldiers], for they were brave men and they were his men."

Lowell himself would die heroically at the Battle of Cedar Creek a year and a half later.

The heroic charge of the 54th quickly became legend in the North. Black enlistment soared. Two weeks after Wagner, Albanus Fisher, a black sergeant of the 54th, wrote "I still feel more Eager for the struggle than I ever yet have, for I now wish to have revenge for our galant Curnel." The 54th fought on and valiantly—at the Battle of Olustee in Florida, men from the 54th, knowing they would be executed if captured, ignored their own safety and used ropes to pull a broken-down train full of wounded soldiers to safety. By the time Lee surrendered at Appomattox, 178,975 black soldiers—including 74 percent of the free black men in the North between eighteen and forty-five years old—had served and more than 37,000 had died in the fight for liberty.

19

James Michael Curley, 1874–1958
Boston's Mayor of the Poor

James Michael Curley watched his young widowed mother wear her knees raw scrubbing the floors of the rich, and it fueled in him a resentment that defined Boston politics for almost half a century.

Clawing his way out of the slums of Ward 17 in Roxbury, using his fists and favors, his wit and his tongue, Curley's life mirrored and magnified the Boston Irish experience—clannish and familial, Catholic and fatalistic, every triumph followed by a tragedy, every tragedy handled with laughter as well as tears.

In 1904, Curley won a seat on Boston's Board of Aldermen while in jail for taking a civil service test for an Irish immigrant friend. Thirty-three years later—during his fourth term as mayor—Curley served five months in a federal penitentiary for mail fraud. "His Honor" ran up deficits and drove the wealthy to the suburbs with tax increases by undertaking huge public building projects, personally negotiating the contracts and always taking a cut for himself. After his death, Boston turned his twenty-one-room mansion in Jamaica Plain—with its marble fireplace and shamrocks carved into all the shutters—into an historical landmark. The joke in the Hub back then was that it was the second time the city had paid for the house.

James Michael Curley

Curley always had a fin or ten-spot in his pocket for those down on their luck. He handed out government jobs to his family and friends, qualifications be damned. When he became governor in 1935, he appointed a grocery salesman to be Commissioner of Agriculture. He tried to appoint Margaret O'Riordan as State Librarian but was turned down by the Governor's Council after reporters interviewed her and she told them the only things she ever read were *Spy Stories* and *True Romance* magazines.

Curley was—and remains to this day—a criminal or a Robin Hood, a saint or a sinner, depending upon whom in Massachusetts you ask. One thing is certain, "the Mayor of the Poor" always got his piece. 'Tis true he ended the corruption of the ward bosses—but he did it by taking their patronage under his personal control. He met with needy constituents every day, finding them jobs or helping them with creditors or police problems—and thus grew an army of friends who owed him favors and votes. Even as a middle-aged man, he was quick with his fists when words failed, which wasn't often since he had, as the Irish say, "the gift of gab." He made thousands of friends and thousands of enemies and, over his long life, many friends became enemies and many enemies became friends. He was larger than life. Frank Skeffington, the protagonist of a best-selling novel, *The Last Hurrah*—published and made into a hit film while Curley was still alive—is often confused with the real man.

His triumphs were matched by his tragedies. His first wife, Mary Herlihy Curley, suffered a lingering death from cancer in 1930—"Mayor Curley's devotion to his wife made even his enemies admire him," the *Boston Herald* opined—and six months later an embolism killed his twenty-three-year-old heir apparent, James Michael Jr. By 1944, five of his nine children had died—twins John and Joseph in infancy, Dorothea at fourteen from pneumonia, and son Paul, a hopeless alcoholic, who passed in his sleep at thirty-two. But nothing could have prepared Curley for February 11, 1950—a month after his final mayoral term ended—when his forty-one-year-old daughter Mary and thirty-four-year-old son Leo both suffered cerebral hemorrhages just hours apart while talking on the same telephone in the same apartment on Beacon Street.

"No matter what you say of him, you have to admire him for his great courage," John F. Kennedy, then a thirty-three-year-old congressman, said to a friend as they left the dual wake in Curley's home the next day. (The future president's grandfather, John F. Fitzgerald, and Curley had been bitter rivals for decades. Curley even blackmailed "Honey Fitz" into abandoning his quest for re-election in 1913 by threatening to reveal the mayor's involvement with Elizabeth "Toodles" Ryan, a voluptuous twenty-three-year-old cigarette girl.)

Political grudges are seldom forgiven in Boston, but they took a backseat that day in 1950. The seventy-five-year-old Curley stood beside his son's and daughter's caskets—Mary laid out in a white party dress and Leo in his naval officer's uniform—greeting Archbishop Richard Cushing, Boston Pops conductor Arthur Fiedler, Boston schoolchildren, and thousands of friends and rivals from around the state who just kept coming and coming through the afternoon and evening.

"Later, as a snowstorm whipped the last of the estimated fifty thousand mourners remaining in line, Curley bent low over Mary's form and kissed her lovingly on the forehead," Jack Beatty wrote in his biography *The Rascal King*. "He was weeping openly now, for the first time that day, and to the people still in line and the newspapermen in the room it was a wrenching moment. He looked with pride at his son's uniform and then kissed him for the last time. Shaking from the effort of suppressing his sobs, he retired to bed, walking slowly up the staircase of his aspirations where he had posed with Mary on her wedding day. It was 11:30. He had stood over their bodies for ten hours. At 1:30 a.m., snow clotting their eyes, a delegation of cleaning women who worked the night shift arrived to pay their respects. Curley had waited for them as long as he could."

Those cleaning women, along with teamsters, laborers, dockworkers, widows, and waitresses, had been his base. Elected four times as Boston mayor, four times to Congress, and once as Massachusetts governor, Curley had become the champion of the immigrant and second-generation Irish— and also of the newly arrived Italians, Jews, and other poor Europeans—by openly fighting a class war with the Boston Brahmins, the elite descendants of the Puritans and Pilgrims who had controlled the city and state since the seventeenth century.

"Even as a boy, I knew I belonged to an Irish-Catholic minority who were despised socially and discriminated against politically," Curley said in his ghostwritten autobiography, *I'd Do it Again*. "I chose politics because industrial conditions were deplorable and prospects of ever getting anywhere seemed remote."

In speech after speech, Curley recalled his people's persecution by the Know-Nothings in 1850's Boston, when the famine Irish were treated as less than human—"leeches" according to one Know-Nothing newspaper—and the majority of the deaths in Boston's Irish ghettos were children under five. Things got better for the Irish in the early twentieth century, but not much better. "Trapped in a declining economy, the Boston Irish needed scapegoats," Beatty wrote. "And they would have them: James Michael Curley would see to that." Curley claimed it was the Irish who made Boston a great city and with a wink—everything was always with a wink—said the Boston Tea Party was really the Boston Beer Party, conceived in a tavern owned by an Irishman. He turned "blue blood" into a curse word in his many us-against-them speeches delivered in a voice described by Beatty as "smooth and rich and it had extraordinary range; in a single sentence, he could shift from baritone to tenor to countertenor."

Curley, a devout Catholic, "appealed to religious as well as class antagonisms," Reinhard H. Luthin wrote in his 1954 book *American Demagogues*. "Once on a South Boston platform, before an Irish-American audience, he ended a speech with the demagogic climax: 'And where was my esteemed opponent when all this was going on? He was in the Ritz Hotel in white tie and tails eating a steak dinner—and on a Friday!'"

In one speech in the Italian North End, Curley said: "Republicans don't want someone to care for babies, the aged and to pay a living wage. They want someone who will sit on the lid, will not spend and will cut down debt. Government was not created to save money and to cut debt, but to take care of people. That's my theory of government."

Curley did take care of people—and himself. "Everybody knew," biographer Joseph Dinneen wrote, "there wasn't a contract awarded that did not carry with it a cut for Curley." He took long vacations in first-class hotels, sent his kids to private schools, bought a yacht, and left big tips. "In this way he spent hundreds of thousands of dollars, much of which he did not earn but took, indirectly, from the working-and lower-middle-class taxpayers of Boston," Beatty wrote. "Yet he said that the title he cherished most was 'the Mayor of the Poor,' and the poor venerated him."

Between 1898 and 1955, Curley ran for office thirty-two times. He served on the Boston City Council and on its predecessors, the Boston Common Council and Board of Aldermen. He was elected to the Massachusetts House of Representatives for one term. He won all but one of his five Congressional races. He ran for mayor ten times and won four times. His last term, 1946–1949, included five months in a federal penitentiary. He ran for governor three times, winning once in 1934, and ran unsuccessfully for the U.S. Senate in 1936 when he glibly called Henry Cabot Lodge Jr., his Brahmin opponent, "Little Boy Blue." Curley will always be remembered as Boston's mayor, but he preferred to be addressed as "Governor."

He died from stomach cancer in 1958. Beatty wrote that after a five-hour operation, Curley momentarily opened his eyes while being wheeled on a gurney, saw reporters and his son Francis there, and, with a wink, said, "Franno, I wish to announce the first plank in my campaign for reelection—we're going to have the floors in this goddamned hospital smoothed out."

Those were his last words. More than 100,000 people attended his wake at the statehouse—including the scrub-women whom he had provided long-handled mops to while governor to get them off their knees. An estimated one million people lined the streets for his funeral procession. The city that once belonged to the Protestant Cabots, Lowells, and Lodges now belonged to the Catholic Irish Americans and two years later one of their own would be elected president. "His triumph was their triumph," the *Boston Herald* said in Curley's obituary. It was a larger than life ending for a larger than life man.

That life began in Boston in 1874, although in many ways it began between 1846 and 1849 when the great potato famine drove tens of thousands of Ireland's sons and daughters to Boston, joining an already swelling Gaelic population in Massachusetts. The Irish in America were poor, uneducated, hated, and misused. By the 1850s, Irish Need Not Apply signs hung on factory doors in the Hub, and Protestant politicians sponsored anti-immigration legislation—under a "pauper removal law" 1,300 of the most desperate Irish in Boston were even shipped back to Liverpool. The Irish in Boston, almost to a man, joined the antireform, antiabolition Democratic Party. Their numbers grew—the Irish were the ethnic majority in the Hub by 1880—but the Yankees and their money still controlled businesses, government, and the press.

Curley's parents, Michael and Sarah, both emigrated from Galway in 1864, married in 1870 and settled in Roxbury's Ward 17, a rough neighborhood of tenements. Sarah gave birth to three sons—John, then James, then Michael, who died at two years old. Curley's thirty-four-year-old father died three years later after picking up a huge stone while working as a laborer. Still in public school and an avid reader, James, then ten, ran errands for a drugstore and grocery to help his mother pay the bills. "He never forgot that at a time when his family desperately needed help they received nothing from the boss of Ward 17, Pea Jacket Maguire—not a box of food nor a visit to the house. Nothing," wrote Doris Kearns Goodwin in her book, *The Fitzgeralds and the Kennedys*.

Before he was twenty, Curley developed political ambitions, became active in the ward and in the church, and joined the fraternal Ancient Order of Hibernians. In 1897, at twenty-three years old, he bought a coat and vest at a store that sold the used clothing of Harvard students and ran for the Ward 17 seat on the Boston Common Council. He narrowly lost. He lost again in 1898 but finally won in 1899. About that time he and his friends formed a Ward 17 social and political organization they called the Tammany Club after the scandal-ridden New York administration. It would soon prove an entirely appropriate name with Curley as the club's perennial president.

"Prominent Ward 17 Democratic politicians suspected of fraud by federal officers," screamed a front-page headline in the *Boston Herald* on Feb. 11, 1903. Curley, by then a state representative, and a fellow politician had taken the civil service test for two recent Irish immigrants who wanted to be postmen. They had been recognized and all four were jailed. Curley admitted during the trial that he had taken the test and used the phrase that would get him elected over and over. "I did it for a friend," he said, for a man who needed the job to feed his wife and kids.

Curley ran a campaign for alderman from his jail cell and won a seat on the 1904 board. By distributing favors and jobs to "friends" and Christmas gifts to Ward 17 children, he easily won a seat as an alderman/city councilor every year after that until 1911. In 1906, he married Mary Herlihy, who also hailed from Ward 17. Their marriage proved strong and he often credited Mary's advice in his decisions. Curley was already playing his "us-against-them" card at every opportunity.

"Between 1900 and 1914, Curley bred unprecedented tumult in Boston politics," Beatty wrote. "He was denounced from pulpits and excoriated by editorialists. Headlines made his name synonymous with scandal. His 'image,' as we would call his reputation today, would never be cleansed of this early taint. And yet without it, his political ascent would not have been possible. For every enemy bad publicity made him, it made him two friends."

Curley had become the standard bearer for the Irish poor and for the entire Boston underclass. He railed against immigration restrictions when he went to Washington following his election in 1911 to Congress, earning him new friends among Massachusetts' burgeoning Italian and Jewish population. His sights were set on becoming mayor, though, and when Mayor John "Honey" Fitzgerald announced he wouldn't run for re-election in 1913, Curley threw his fedora into the ring along with eight other candidates. Seven of Boston's nine daily newspapers promptly editorialized against him.

Honey Fitz briefly re-entered the campaign but threats by Curley to reveal his involvement with Elizabeth Ryan— Curley even placed a notice in the newspapers of a lecture series he planned that included "Great Lovers from Cleopatra to Toodles"— forced Fitzgerald out of the race. Curley then faced Thomas Kenny of South Boston, also an Irishman but the candidate of the Yankee-controlled Good Government Association, or "Goo Goos" as Curley called them. "There has been no man in my experience on the city government who has shown less capacity and whose record in public life is more questionable than that of Mr. Curley," Kenny, a respected lawyer, said.

Curley beat Kenny by less than six thousand votes of the eighty thousand cast but the era of the Purple Shamrock had begun. He lost in 1917—although he kept Honey Fitz out of that race simply by suggesting he still might give his "Great Lovers" lecture—but won again in 1921, 1929, and 1945. In between his mayoral stints, he served as president of the Hibernia Savings Bank, as governor from 1935 to 1937, and as congressman again from 1943 to 1947.

On his last day as governor, he married a widow named Gertrude Casey Dennis. As the couple left the statehouse ten thousand admirers stood in a cold rain to see them drive off in a new Lincoln while a band played "Till We Meet Again."

Love him or hate him, there was no middle ground. In a 1984 essay, historian Charles Trout argued that Curley never received his due as a great progressive. Lost in his quotable inauguration threat to sell Boston Common, and in his quips about the Yankees tracing family lineage that could "easily have proven that they sailed with Captain Kidd or with some other man equally honest," there lived a true reformer.

"His record in the City Council, as a Congressman, and as Mayor of Boston should have earned him accolades from anyone who cared about the broader contours of social justice," Trout wrote. "Whenever a department head removed an elderly worker to make room for someone younger, Curley went to the barricades against 'the kind of economy that drives [the superannuated] to the poor house . . . and makes of them a public charge.'"

In addition to initiating public projects that included vocational high schools, bridges, tunnels, beaches, and roads—and provided jobs to be given out—Curley advocated pensions for city workers and the creation of a statewide old-age assistance program. He supported better benefits for government workers and the labor unions. He demanded mentally-disabled patients in the Fernald School be given pillows. He fought to maintain the nickel fare on all streetcars and subways and he opposed construction of elevated train lines as a noisy blight on neighborhoods. He became more and more reckless with taking his cuts and helping his cronies over the years, however, and "more given to demagogic appeals," as Trout put it. He never won a statewide election other than the gubernatorial contest in 1934 during the depths of the Great Depression.

In 1947, during his last term as mayor and still holding his seat in Congress, the seventy-two-year-old Curley was jailed again—this time in the federal penitentiary in Danbury,

Connecticut, for mail fraud—until President Harry Truman commuted the sentence and later gave him a complete pardon. He was welcomed back to Boston like a conquering hero but promptly made a new enemy when he claimed he did more work in his first five days back than his stand-in, John B. Hynes, did in five months. Hynes, who had actually done all the work, wouldn't forgive him for that slight and narrowly beat Curley in the next mayoral election. Curley challenged him again in 1951 and lost.

"Any number of progressives and, later, liberal Democrats thought him tainted," Trout wrote. "He would forever be the 'Jailbird Mayor of Boston'. . . . By the end of his life, he had retreated into the identity picked up by [author] Edwin O'Connor in *The Last Hurrah*, a portrait that does not do him justice."

Curley had become by 1954 a national punch line to any joke about cronyism and official corruption. Luthin wrote that year in *American Demagogues,* "The voters . . . felt nostalgia for the old-time pugnacious politician, but they also felt embarrassment."

The "Mayor of the Poor," at eighty-one years old and crushed by the weight of his own legacy, ran half-heartedly once more in 1955 but lost in the primary. Three years later, Curley had a true last hurrah when one hundred thousand people filed past his casket in the statehouse.

"The biggest wake was followed by the biggest funeral," Beatty wrote. "A crowd of one million, in the impeachable estimates of the police, lined the sidewalks to watch the hearse carrying James Michael Curley pass through the streets of the city he had led and to which he had given life and laughter, sorrow and scandal, for over fifty years. . . . For the Irish Americans among them, especially, he was a political and cultural hero, an axial figure in their annals. He had lived for them."

20

---◆---

Major Taylor, 1878–1932
The Worcester Whirlwind

By the time he was thirteen, Marshall "Major" Taylor had already won a gold medal competing against white men in a bicycle race in his native Indianapolis.

Less than four years later, Jim Crow segregation laws would bar him from races and drive Taylor out of that city. Even though he found Worcester, his adopted hometown, an oasis of tolerance compared to Indiana, prejudice still ran deep against the "little colored boy" who had the talent and the will to be the fastest bicycle racer in the world—which, from 1898 to 1904, he was.

By the time he was nineteen, white racers across the Northeast and Midwest had forced him to crash into fences, thrown buckets of cold water into his face, and tossed nails at his tires, boxed him in—pocketing it was called—and made "white-only" rules for their organizations in an attempt to keep him out of racing altogether. After one race in Taunton in 1897, third-place finisher William Becker pulled the slender Taylor off his bike and strangled him into unconsciousness. Becker was not suspended for his attack and his fellow white racers even chipped in to pay his $50 fine.

Still Major Taylor persevered, beating all comers with his courage, athleticism, and intelligence. He set dozens of records and won a world championship—all against a backdrop of

LA VIE AU GRAND AIR

ABONNEMENTS · 10 Mars 1901. — N° 130 · PUBLICITÉ

Rédaction et Administration : 370, rue Saint-Honoré, PARIS (1er Arr°).

MAJOR TAYLOR

Le célèbre sprinter noir, champion de vitesse d'Amérique, qui arrivera à Paris dans quelques jours pour se mesurer avec les plus fameux coureurs européens.

Front page of a Parisian sports magazine

unparalleled prejudice in America. (More lynchings occurred in the 1890s than in any other decade.) A half a century before Jackie Robinson broke the color line in professional baseball, even before heavyweight Jack Johnson's celebrated triumphs in the ring, the "Worcester Whirlwind" prevailed in the most popular sport of the time—so popular that its stars, including Taylor, could earn thousands of dollars in a single day while future Hall of Fame baseball players like Ty Cobb earned less than $5,000 in a year. Tens of thousands of spectators would attend races in Madison Square Garden and in more than fifty velodromes on the East Coast. Bike racing was huge—the velodrome in Newark, New Jersey, held twenty-five thousand spectators.

Although despised by jealous white racers—who considered him their social inferior—the pluck and heart of the skinny 5-foot-7 black kid who darted through the narrowest of openings made him a fan favorite and a great draw for promoters. Newspaper reporters, in the style of the day, came up with one nickname after another—the "Colored Cyclone," the "Worcester Whirlwind," the "Ebony Streak"—as Taylor pedaled to win after win, despite muggings, pocketing, and other tactics attempted to deny him victories.

More important than his records and championships in the face of what he called "that monster prejudice," is the way Taylor accomplished those victories—always as a sportsman. From 1896 until 1909, the deeply religious, teetotaling Baptist lost out on tens of thousands of dollars because he wouldn't race on Sundays. His life became a tragedy after racing. His wife left him and he lost touch with his daughter. He lost his house in Worcester and all of his money through bad investments. Although he was a brilliant mechanic, he was denied admission to all-white Worcester Polytechnic Institute after his racing career ended, ostensibly because he didn't have a high school diploma. Painful shingles caused by a frayed nervous system repeatedly hospitalized him. He spent years writing a 431-page autobiography, which he then self-published and tried to sell from the trunk of his car with little success.

Trials that even Job might break under, but Taylor never lost faith.

"I hold no animosity towards any man," Taylor wrote toward the end of his book, *The Fastest Bicycle Rider in the World*. "This includes those who so bitterly opposed me and did everything possible to injure me and prevent my success. . . . When I am finally run off my feet and flattened by that mighty champion Father Time, the last thought to remain in my mind will be that throughout life's great race, I always gave the best that was in me. Life is too short for a man to hold bitterness in his heart. As the late Booker T. Washington, the great Negro educator, so beautifully expressed it, 'I shall allow no man to narrow my soul and drag me down, by making me hate him.'"

If anyone had a cause to hate or to be bitter about the way his life worked out, it was Taylor. In 1930, a year after writing that passage, a destitute Taylor left Worcester, his home of thirty-five years. He filled his car with his books and drove to Chicago, where a quarter century earlier he had won rich races before thousands of adoring fans. The Great Depression had already started, however, and few in Chicago, even if they had been inclined, could afford to buy his book. He wound up living alone in a YMCA and then died in the charity ward of Cook County Hospital. He was buried in a pauper's grave in Mount Glenwood Cemetery.

"The golden age of American bicycle racing has receded into the past until it exists as only a faint memory," Taylor's biographer Andrew Ritchie wrote in 1988. "Occasionally, an article appears in a cycling magazine or a Worcester or Indianapolis newspaper reminding readers of an outstanding pioneer black athlete called Major Taylor . . . [who] deserves to emerge from the shadows where he has languished for so long."

Taylor was born on November 26, 1878, on a small farm outside Indianapolis. His grandparents had been slaves in neighboring Kentucky and Taylor's father had fought with an all-black regiment in the Civil War. When Marshall Taylor was eight, his father took a job as coachman for the Southards, a wealthy white family. The Southards had just one child, a boy named Daniel, and "I was eventually employed as his playmate . . . we were kept dressed just alike all the time," Taylor wrote in his autobiography. "The rest of Dan's playmates were of wealthy families . . . all the boys owned bicycles, excepting myself, but Dan saw to it that I had one too."

Taylor moved in with the Southards for several years and benefited from a private tutor and all the other trappings of wealth. Living with the Southards "expanded his horizons enormously, and gave him great expectations." Ritchie wrote. "He learned to measure himself against his white playmates and understood he was their physical equal."

In the early 1890s, the Southards moved to Chicago but left Marshall a bicycle. He learned to do stunts on it and the next year, when he was thirteen, he was hired to do tricks in front of the Hays & Willits bike shop. While performing, Taylor wore a military uniform with shiny buttons—thus the nickname Major. The trick riding paid handsome dividends in his later racing years, according to Todd Balf, the author of 2008's *Major: A Black Athlete, A White Era, and the Fight to Be the World's Fastest Human Being*. "He could do virtually anything on a bike and it gave him supreme confidence in what was a fast, physical, and highly intense sport," Balf said.

That same year, 1892, Taylor won his first race and soon hooked up with Louis "Birdie" Munger, a star racer back in the days of high-wheel bicycles, who had become a manufacturer in the booming bike industry. Taylor worked in Munger's bike shop and became his valet of sorts and his protégé, and through him met many of the current stars of pro bike racing. Munger had grown up in Ontario, Canada, in a community where one-third of the residents were black.

"When he met Taylor . . . and then began to brag about him as a prospective world champion, it was as if he was foolishly naive and didn't understand the harsh, racially tinted lens through which all of America seemed to be staring—and he didn't," Balf wrote. "He was from a much different part of the world, a mere few miles from the border that divided Canada from the United States but an incalculable distance away from the notion that a black man was born inferior to a white one."

In 1895, when he was sixteen, Taylor rode one of Munger's ultra-light bikes to victory in a seventy-mile race from Indianapolis to Matthews, Indiana. All the other riders quit because of a downpour, and also because of the huge lead Taylor quickly raced out to. A year earlier, bicycle racing's organizing body, the League of American Wheelmen, banned blacks from membership. "Why should [the League] admit one with whom not one of its members would dance at a public or private ball?" a columnist in *Referee*, a bicycle trade journal, concurred. The League did rule that nonmember blacks could enter races, but white promoters in Indianapolis, in the days of Jim Crow segregation, often balked. Taylor wasn't even allowed to train at the YMCA in his native city. In desperation, Munger tried to bleach Taylor's skin with a mixture of chemicals, but feared it would poison his protégé and stopped after a few days.

Partially because of business, and partially because Munger was convinced Taylor could be the fastest bicyclist in the world, he decided to move his factory to Worcester, a manufacturing city in central Massachusetts with a small black population but a long history of pre–Civil War abolition.

"I was in Worcester only a very short time before I realized that there was no such race prejudice existing among the bicycle riders there as I had experienced in Indianapolis," Taylor later wrote.

The City of Seven Hills became a great place for Taylor to train—and not just because he could join the Y. Even today, bicyclists emulate Taylor by pedaling up George Street, two blocks with a 23 percent grade. Of course, they have multiple gears now. Taylor had just one.

Taylor, still an amateur in 1896, was soon winning races everywhere he went. He and Munger returned to Indianapolis to race on a new track where Taylor, paced by riders on tandem bikes, shattered the mile record by more than eight seconds and also set a new one-fifth mile record. White riders were furious.

"Even though he had beaten only the times of the white riders, not raced with them, Taylor's rides were seen as a provocation, an attempt to stir up trouble," Ritchie wrote. "He was banned thereafter from that particular track."

Taylor turned pro in 1897. He won $100 in his first race by beating the reigning sprint champion, Eddie Bald, in a duel at Madison Square Garden, with the crowd cheering wildly for the "dusky wheelman." He then took part in the Six Day, a nonstop test of endurance in which riders would ride for hours and hours, take a short rest, and get back on. They'd even eat as they pedaled. Twelve thousand spectators packed the Garden on the sixth day to witness the spectacle as riders became almost psychotic from lack of sleep. The winner who covered the most miles won $5,000. Only twelve men finished—Taylor placed eighth.

The newspaper reporters and most fans loved him, but even in the relatively liberal Northeast, Taylor faced great racism, particularly from other riders. The month before Becker choked him in Taunton, another rider intentionally drove him into a fence in Worcester and Taylor was badly cut up. In New Jersey, white riders threatened to kill him.

"I have a dread of injury every time I start in a race with the men who have been on the circuit this year," Taylor told the *Worcester Telegram*.

The racism was even worse in the South. Promoters there refused to let him compete in late 1897, costing him the National Sprint Championship. Southern newspapers called him the "coon racer" and worse. He and his trainer had to flee Georgia the following winter after Taylor challenged three whites on a triplet to a race on a Savannah street after one snarled at him that they didn't "pace niggers." The next day, Taylor and his trainer received written death threats—"Clear out if you value your life." They did.

In 1898, Taylor continued to set records, win races, and make money. He also continually faced discrimination—in hotels and restaurants and in races. In 1899, he won twenty-two major races plus the World Championship in Montreal. He broke his own record in the mile twice. In 1900, he won the American Sprint Championship and turned down offers of $10,000 and $15,000 to race in France because he would not race on Sundays. (He said he would not out of respect for the Sabbath and his late mother's wishes. "I honestly believe in the saying, 'A mother's prayer will last forever,'" he told reporters.)

The twenty-one-year-old Taylor, who was quickly becoming one of the richest black men in America, bought a new house in Worcester's affluent Columbus Park neighborhood. White neighbors were upset and offered to buy the house for $2,000 more than he had paid. Taylor refused and moved in with one of his sisters.

Finally, in 1901, a new offer came from France—$7,200 for a four-month tour with no Sunday racing. Taylor was a huge hit in Europe, beating every European champion and winning forty-two of the fifty-seven races he rode in. In France, where bicycle racing is still the national sport, they called him "le Negre Volant"—the Flying Negro.

"In his own country he was a persona non grata," Ritchie wrote, "but from the moment he arrived in France, he was a *cause celebre*, the long-awaited, much publicized champion." An article in *Le Velo*, a Paris-based bicycling magazine, called Taylor, "a Messiah."

"One must always bear in mind that he is black and that he has done all his racing in America," another article in *Le Velo* said. "Each victory of Taylor's has been won against all the rest of the riders. . . . The Negro was the enemy who absolutely had to be beaten."

Taylor toured Europe and Australia almost continuously for the next three years with an occasional brief rest in Worcester. In March 1902, he married Daisy Morris, the wealthy, cultured daughter of a black woman and white man, and the new Mrs. Taylor accompanied her husband abroad, where they were treated like royalty most of the time. He returned home for the American championships in 1902 and competed, but, once again, his white rivals conspired to pocket him and prevented him from winning. "With . . . the honest observation of the rules of bicycle racing, Major Taylor would be Champion of America again," one New York newspaper wrote. In 1903, Taylor said he would never race in America again. He talked about retiring altogether but signed a lucrative contract for one more Australian tour where he would compete against two of his most bitter, racist American rivals, Iver Lawson and Floyd McFarland. In Melbourne, Lawson intentionally caused a crash that injured Taylor and was suspended and left the country. In 1904, Daisy gave birth to a daughter in Sydney. The Taylors named their only child Rita Sydney.

Taylor, only twenty-seven, retired in 1905 and spent the next two years at home and driving around the city in his car, one of the few in Worcester. In 1907, he signed on for another European tour. Older and out-of-shape he performed poorly at first but had regained some abilities by the end of the tour. His comeback continued through 1908 and 1909, although he was no longer the star he had once been and had to agree to race on Sundays. He missed his wife and daughter, the injuries healed more slowly, and he finally retired in 1910.

Over the next twenty years, Taylor became involved in several businesses, all of which failed, and his status in the Worcester community steadily declined. He eventually became an auto tire repairman. He did ride once more, taking part in an old-timers' race in Newark in 1917. His old manager, Birdie Munger, drove all night to be his starter. Taylor won the race, the only race he ever rode on a Sunday in America.

In the early 1920s, Taylor began to write his autobiography, "in the spirit calculated to solicit simple justice, equal rights and a square deal for the prosperity of my downtrodden but brave people." He also needed money. He had been selling property and his wife's jewelry to pay bills. Then he sickened and his constant battle with shingles, which worsened with stress, caused him to sell his home. He and Daisy moved into an apartment. She began working two jobs to pay for Sydney's college tuition. The *Worcester Telegram*, upon learning of Taylor's hardships, ran an appeal that raised $1,200 in a week. ("Worcester World Champion . . . Now Among the Needy," said the headline.)

In 1929, Taylor finished his 431-page autobiography, which included poetry and advice on healthy living and, despite a litany of his on-and off-track persecutions, ultimately contains an uplifting message.

"There are positively no mental, physical, moral or other attainments too lofty for a Negro to accomplish if granted a fair and equal opportunity," Taylor wrote.

He could not find a publisher so he self-published his book, another expensive venture. He sold it door-to-door in Worcester and around New England from the trunk of his car without much success. In 1930, after twenty-eight years of marriage, Daisy left Taylor and moved to New York. Sydney had already moved to New Orleans. A broken man, Taylor drove to Chicago. The Great Depression was on and he had no success there. He ended up living at a YMCA and died alone in a charity ward from heart problems on June 21, 1932. Daisy and Sydney did not learn of his death until weeks later, after Major Taylor had been buried in an unmarked pauper's grave.

He remained there, forgotten, for sixteen years until a group of ex-professional racers, with the aid of the Schwinn Bicycle Company, exhumed his body and reburied it under a bronze plaque that says: "World champion bicycle racer who came up the hard way, without hatred in his heart, an honest courageous and God-fearing, clean-living gentlemanly athlete.

A credit to his race who always gave his best. Gone but not forgotten."

In fact, he was mostly forgotten for three more decades. In 1982, though, the City of Indianapolis named a new track after Taylor and, in 1988, Ritchie's biography stimulated new, widespread interest in the groundbreaking champion. Riding teams across the country—especially black teams—adopted the name Major Taylor.

In Worcester, journalist Lynne Tolman joined the newly formed Major Taylor Association in the 1990s and tirelessly spearheaded a ten-year effort to erect a fitting monument to the Worcester Whirlwind. In 2006, the city renamed Worcester Center Boulevard as Major Taylor Boulevard, and on May 21, 2008, a ten-foot-high bronze statue of Major Taylor—sculptor Toby Mendez used a young black bike racer from Indianapolis as his model—was unveiled in front of Worcester Public Library. Three-time Tour de France winner Greg LeMond and three-time Olympic gold medalist Edwin Moses spoke. Major Taylor's relatives, including his great-granddaughter, Jan Brown, were among the hundreds who attended.

"What a wonderful day this was," Brown told an audience at the library that night. "And what a wonderful new day this is."

Bibliography

Thomas Morton

Adams, Charles Francis, *Three Episodes of Massachusetts History*. New York and Boston: Houghton Mifflin, 1892.

Bolton, Charles Knowles, *The Real Founders of New England: Stories of Their Life along the Coast, 1602–1628*. Boston: F.W. Faxon Co., 1929.

Bradford, William, *The History of Plimoth Plantation, 1620–1647*. Circa 1650.

Morton, Thomas, *New English Canaan*. Amsterdam, 1637. Edited and annotated with biography by Jack Dempsey. Scituate, Mass.: Digital Scanning Inc., 1999.

Southwick, Albert B., "Early settler loved New England, not Puritans, Pilgrims" Worcester, Mass.: *Telegram & Gazette*. Apr 23, 2006.

Anne Hutchinson

Adams, Charles Francis, *Three Episodes of Massachusetts History*. New York: Houghton Mifflin, 1892.

Humphrey, Grace, *Women in American History*. Indianapolis: The Bobbs-Merrill Company, 1919.

Hutchinson, Thomas, *History of the Colony and Province of Massachusetts*. Boston, 1767. Edited by Lawrence Shaw Mayo. Cambridge: Harvard University Press, 1936.

LaPlante, Eve, *American Jezebel: The Uncommon Life of Anne Hutchinson, the Woman Who Defied the Puritans*. New York: Harper, 2004.

Rugg, Winnifred King, *Unafraid: A Life of Anne Hutchinson*. New York: Houghton Mifflin, 1930.

Metacom, aka King Philip

Lepore, Jill, *The Name of War, King Philip's War and the Origins of American Identity*. New York: Alfred A. Knopf, 1998.

Mather, Increase, *An History of the Warr with Indians in New England*. London, 1676. Paul Royster editor of online Electronic Text Edition in 2006.

Moynihan, Kenneth J., *The History of Worcester*. Charlestown, S.C.: The History Press, 2007.

Rowlandson, Mary, *The Sovereignty and Goodness of God, The Narrative of the Captivity and the Restoration of Mrs. Mary Rowlandson*. Cambridge, Mass.: 1682.

Schultz, Eric B. and Michael Tougias, *King Philip's War: The History and Legacy of America's Forgotten Conflict*. Woodstock, Vermont: Countryman Press, 1999.

Samuel Adams

Cushing, Harry Alonzo, ed., *The Writings of Samuel Adams*. New York: G.P. Putnam's Sons, 1904.

Eddlem, Thomas, "Father of the American Revolution: Pious, Principled, and Passionate for Liberty, Samuel Adams Championed the Cause of Independence with His Unique Ability to Communicate, Motivate, and Organize." *The New American,* Vol. 18, July 29, 2002.

Goodrich, Rev. Charles A., *Lives of the Signers to the Declaration of Independence*. New York: Thomas Mather, 1829.

Green, Harry Clinton and Mary Wolcott Green, *The Pioneer Mothers of America*. New York : G.P. Putnam's Sons, 1912.

Hosmer, James Kendall, *Samuel Adams*. New York: Houghton Mifflin, 1885.

McCullough, David, *John Adams*. New York: Simon & Schuster, 2001.

Smith, Gary Scott, "The Indispensable Man, *The Washington Times*, July 4, 2007.

Daniel Shays

Dewey, Chester and Field, David, *A History of the County of Berkshire, Massachusetts*. Pittsfield: Samuel W. Bush, 1829.

Starkey, Marion L., *A Little Rebellion*. New York: Alfred A. Knopf, 1955.

Szatmary, David P., *Shays' Rebellion: The Making of an Agrarian Insurrection*. Ann Arbor, Mich.: University of Massachusetts Press, 1980.

Vidal, Gore, *Inventing A Nation*. New Haven: Yale University Press, 2003.

Isaiah Thomas

Brigham, Clarence, *Journals and Journeymen: A Contribution to the History of Early American Newspapers*. Philadelphia: University of Pennsylvania Press, 1950.

Hudson, Frederic, *Journalism in the United States, from 1690–1872*. New York: Harper & Brothers, 1873.

Thomas, Isaiah, *The History of Printing in America: with a Biography of Printers & an Account of Newspapers*. Worcester, 1810, republished with additions and memoir by Benjamin Franklin Thomas, American Antiquarian Society, 1874.

Williams, Julie Hedgepeth, *The Significance of the Printed Word in Early America: Colonists' Thoughts on the Role of the Press*. Westport, Conn.: Greenwood Press, 1999.

Deborah Samson

Campbell, Karlyn Kohrs, *Women Public Speakers in the United States, 1800–1925*. Westport, Conn.: Greenwood Press, 1993.

Mann, Herman, *The Female Review; Or, Memoirs of An American Lady*. Dedham, Mass.: Printed by Nathaniel and Benjamin Heaton for the author, 1797.

Wright, Richardson, *Forgotten Ladies: Nine Portraits from the American Family Album*. Philadelphia: J.B. Lippincott Company, 1928.

Young, Alfred, *Masquerade: The Life and Times of Deborah Sampson, Continental Soldier*. New York: Alfred A. Knopf, 2004.

William Miller

Abanes, Richard, *End-Time Visions: The Road to Armageddon?* New York: Four Walls, Eight Windows, 1998.

Bliss, Sylvester, *Memoirs of William Miller.* Boston: Joshua V. Himes, 1853, republished by Andrews University Press, Berrien Springs, Mich.: 2006.

Brekus, Catherine A., *Strangers & Pilgrims: Female Preaching in America, 1740–1845*. Chapel Hill: University of North Carolina Press, 1998.

Conkin, Paul K., *American Originals: Homemade Varieties of Christianity*. Chapel Hill: University of North Carolina Press, 1997.

O'Leary, Stephen D., *Arguing the Apocalypse: A Theory of Millennial Rhetoric*. New York: Oxford University Press, 1998.

Sears, Clara Endicott, *Days of Delusion*. Cambridge, Mass.: The Riverside Press, 1924.

Joseph Palmer

Holbrook, Stewart, "The Beard of Joseph Palmer," *The American Scholar*, Autumn 1944. 455-458.

No author cited: Interview with Thomas Palmer *Boston Daily Globe,*1884, as quoted in *Bronson Alcott's Fruitlands*, 1915.

No author cited. "Wore A Beard . . . And was Persecuted in the Long Ago." Leominster, Mass.: *Leominster Enterprise*, July 2, 1901.

Sears, Clara Endicott, *Bronson Alcott's Fruitlands*, with *Transcendental Wild Oats* by Louisa May Alcott, Cambridge and Boston: Houghton Mifflin and The Riverside Press, 1915.

Swift, Lindsay, *Brook Farm: Its Members, Scholars and Visitors*. New York: Macmillan, 1900.

Wallace, Irving, "The Hair Piece" *Ramparts Magazine*, February, 1973.

David Walker

Berson, Robin Kadison, *Marching to a Different Drummer: Unrecognized Heroes of American History*. Westport, Conn.: Greenwood Press, 1994.

Greenberg, Kenneth S., *Nat Turner: A Slave Rebellion in History and Memory*. New York: Oxford University Press, 2003.

Horton, James Oliver and Lois E. Horton, *Black Bostonians: Family Life and Community Struggle in the Antebellum North*. New York: Holmes & Meier, 1999.

Miller, Randall M., John R. McKivigan, and Jon L. Wakelyn, *The Moment of Decision: Biographical Essays on American Character and Regional Identity*. Westport, Conn.: Greenwood Press, 1994.

Powell, William S., ed., *Dictionary of North Carolina Biography*. Chapel Hill: University of North Carolina Press, 1979–1996.

Scriven, Darryl, *A Dealer of Old Clothes: Philosophical Conversations with David Walker*. Lanham, Mary. Lexington Books, 2007.

Walker, David, *David Walker's Appeal in Four Articles; Together with a Preamble, to the Coloured Citizens of the World, but in Particular, and Very Expressly, to Those of the United States of America* with a brief sketch of his life by Henry Highland Garnet. Boston: J.H. Tobitt, 1848.

Horace Mann

Compayre, Gabriel, *Horace Mann and the Public School in the United States*. New York: Thomas Y. Crowell & Co., 1907.

Hubbell, George Allen, *Horace Mann, Educator, Patriot and Reformer: A Study in Leadership*. Philadelphia: W.F. Fell, 1910.

Mann, Horace, *A Few Thoughts for a Young Man*. Boston: Ticknor, Reed and Fields, 1850.

Massachusetts Department of Education, *Horace Mann Centennial: 1837–1937*. Boston: Walter A. Smith, 1937.

McCluskey, Neil Gerard, *Public Schools and Moral Education: The Influence of Horace Mann, William Torrey Harris, and John Dewey*. New York: Columbia University Press, 1958.

Stabler, Ernest, *Founders: Innovators in Education 1830–1980*. Edmonton: University of Alberta Press, 1987.

Vinovskis, Maris A., *Education, Society, and Economic Opportunity, A Historical Perspective on Persistent Issues*. New Haven: Yale University Press, 1995.

Winship, Albert E., *Horace Mann: The Educator*. Boston: New England Publishing Co., 1896.

Dorothea Lynde Dix

Brown, Thomas J., *Dorothea Dix: New England Reformer*. Cambridge: Harvard University Press, 1998.

Carman, Harry J. and Harold C. Syrett, *A History of the American People*. New York: Alfred A. Knopf, 1952.

Cimbala, Paul A. and Randall M. Miller, eds., *Against the Tide: Women Reformers in American Society*. Westport, Conn.: Praeger Publishers, 1997.

Dix, Dorothea Lynde, *Memorial to the Massachusetts Legislature*, 1843.

Dix, Dorothea Lynde, *Remarks on Prisons and Prison Discipline in the United States*, 1845, with a new introduction by Leonard D. Savitz. Montclair, N.J.: Patterson Smith, 1967.

Hindus, Michael Stephen, *Prison and Plantation: Crime, Justice, and Authority in Massachusetts and South Carolina, 1767–1878*. Chapel Hill: University of North Carolina Press, 1980.

Tiffany, Francis, *Life of Dorothea Lynde Dix*. New York: Houghton Mifflin, 1890.

Tinling, Marion, *Women Remembered: A Guide to Landmarks of Women's History in the United States*. Westport, Conn.: Greenwood Press, 1986.

Margaret Fuller

Bell, Margaret, *Margaret Fuller, a Biography*. New York: Charles Boni, 1930.

Chipperfield, Faith, *In Quest of Love: The Life and Death of Margaret Fuller*. New York: Coward-McCann, 1957.

Fuller, Margaret, *Summer on the Lakes in 1843*. Urbana: University of Illinois Press, 1991, reprint of 1844 edition.

Miller, Perry, ed., *Margaret Fuller, American Romantic: a Selection from her Writings and Correspondence*. Ithaca: Cornell University Press, 1970.

Von Mehren, Joan, *Minerva and the Muse: A Life of Margaret Fuller*. Amherst, Mass.: University of Massachusetts Press, 1994.

Elihu Burritt

Allen, Devere, *The Fight for Peace*. New York: Macmillan, 1930.

Curti, Merle and Dwight Morrow, *The Learned Blacksmith: The Letters and Journals of Elihu Burritt*. New York, Wilson-Erickson Inc., 1937.

True, Michael, *Worcester Area Writers, 1680–1980*. Worcester, Mass.: Worcester Public Library, 1987.

Henry David Thoreau

Cain, William E., *A Historical Guide to Henry David Thoreau*. New York: Oxford University Press, 2000.

Channing, William Ellery and F. B. Sanborn, editor, *Thoreau, the Poet Naturalist: With Memorial Verses*. New York: Biblo and Tannen, 1966.

Harding, Walter, *Thoreau, Man of Concord*. New York: Holt Rinehart and Winston, 1960.

Thoreau, Henry David, "Civil Disobedience," an
    essay originally published as "Resistance to Civil
    Government," Concord, Mass., 1849.
Thoreau, Henry David, *Walden; or, Life in the Woods*. Boston:
    Ticknor and Fields, 1854.

Lucy Stone
Blackwell, Alice Stone, *Lucy Stone, Pioneer of Woman's Rights*.
    Boston: Little, Brown, and Company, 1930.
Griffith, Elisabeth, *In Her Own Right: The Life of Elizabeth
    Cady Stanton*.New York: Oxford University Press, 1984.
Kerr, Andrea Moore, *Lucy Stone: Speaking out for Equality*.
    New Brunswick, N.J.: Rutgers University Press, 1992.

Helen Hunt Jackson
Coultrap-McQuin, Susan, *Doing Literary Business: American
    Women Writers in the Nineteenth Century*. Chapel Hill:
    University of North Carolina Press, 1990.
Dando-Collins, Stephen, *Standing Bear is a Person*.
    Cambridge, Mass.: Da Capo Press, 2004.
Jackson, Helen Hunt, *A Century of Dishonor*. New York:
    Harper & Brothers, 1881.
Knight, Denise D. and Emmanuel S. Nelson, eds.,
    *Nineteenth-Century American Women Writers: A Bio-
    Bibliographical Critical Sourcebook*. Westport, Conn.:
    Greenwood Press, 1997.
Mathes, Valerie Sherer and Richard Lowitt, *The Standing
    Bear Controversy, Prelude to Indian Reform*. Urbana:
    University of Illinois Press, 2003.
Odell, Ruth, *Helen Hunt Jackson (H.H.)*. New York: D.
    Appleton-Century Company, 1939.
Prucha, Francis Paul, *The Great Father: The United States
    Government and the American Indians*. Lincoln:
    University of Nebraska Press, 1984.

Robert Gould Shaw

Catton, Bruce and James McPherson, *The American Heritage New History of the Civil War*. New York: Viking Penguin, 1996.

Duncan, Russell, *Blue-Eyed Child of Fortune: The Civil War Letters of Colonel Robert Gould Shaw*. Athens, Ga.: University of Georgia Press, 1992.

Golay, Michael, *A Ruined Land: The End of the Civil War*. New York: Wiley, 1999.

Perry, Bliss, *Life and Letters of Henry Lee Higginson*. Boston: Atlantic Monthly Press, 1921.

Robert Gould Shaw. Lithograph, no date. From *Portraits of American Abolitionists*. Massachusetts Historical Society.

Shackel, Paul A., *Memory in Black and White: Race, Commemoration, and the Post-Bellum Landscape*. Walnut Creek, Calif.: Altamira, 2003.

Stewart, William R., *The Philanthropic Work of Josephine Shaw Lowell*. New York: The Macmillan Company, 1911.

Urwin, Gregory J. W., *Black Flag over Dixie: Racial Atrocities and Reprisals in the Civil War*. Carbondale: Southern Illinois University Press, 2004.

Wilson, Keith P., *Campfires of Freedom: The Camp Life of Black Soldiers during the Civil War*. Kent, Ohio.: Kent State University Press, 2002.

James Michael Curley

Beatty, Jack, *The Rascal King: The Life and Times of James Michael Curley, 1874–1958*. Reading, Mass.: Addison Wesley (Current Publisher: Perseus Publishing), 1992.

Connolly, Michael C., "The First Hurrah: James Michael Curley versus the 'Goo-Goos' in the Boston Mayoralty Election of 1914," Essay in *Historical Journal of Massachusetts*, Winter 2002.

Curley, James Michael, *I'd Do It Again: A Record of All My Uproarious Years*. Englewood Cliffs, N.J., Prentice-Hall, 1957.

Dineen, Joseph F., *The Purple Shamrock: The Hon. James Michael Curley of Boston*. New York, W. W. Norton & Co., 1949.

Goodwin, Doris Kearns, *The Fitzgeralds and the Kennedys: An American Saga*. New York: St. Martins, 1991.

Luthin, Reinhard H., *American Demagogues: Twentieth Century*. Boston: Beacon Press, 1954.

Trout, Charles, Essay in *Boston, 1700–1980: The Evolution of Urban Politics* by Ronald P. Formisano and Constance K. Burns. Westport, Conn.: Greenwood Press, 1984.

Major Taylor

Balf, Todd, *Major: A Black Athlete, a White Era, and the Fight to Be the World's Fastest Human Being*. New York: Crown Publishers, 2008.

Brill, Marlene Tagg, *Marshall "Major" Taylor, World Champion Bicyclist, 1899–1901*. Minneapolis: Twenty-First Century Books, 2007.

Ritchie, Andrew, *Major Taylor: The Extraordinary Career of a Champion Bicycle Racer*. Baltimore: Johns Hopkins University Press, 1988.

Taylor, Marshall "Major", *The Fastest Bicycle Rider in the World: The Autobiography of Major Taylor*. Self-published, Worcester, 1928.

Index

About the Author

Massachusetts native Paul Della Valle is a journalist, author, bluegrass songwriter, and musician. He founded and formerly published the *Lancaster Times* and *Clinton Courier* newspapers. He is the creative writing teacher at Mary E. Wells Middle School in Southbridge and an adjunct faculty member of the Northeastern University School of Journalism in Boston. He lives on an old farm in Sterling with his family and their dog, Yaz.